TO THE LAST BREATH

ROSE KRYZAK AND THE
SENIOR ACTION MOVEMENT
IN
NEW YORK STATE

1972-2001

MICHAEL BURGESS

Old age is honored
on the condition
that it defends itself,
maintains its rights,
is subservient to no one,
and to the last breath,
rules over its own domain.

Cicero

*This book is dedicated to the all those
who sail against the wind
and often against public opinion,
working without adequate funding
for social justice for the poor, children,
working families and the elderly*

CONTENTS

Foreword 1

The Birth of the Senior Action Movement 5

Rose Kryzak —
Born with The Century 19

Heat or Eat: The Energy Crisis and
Older New Yorkers in the 1970s 25

Albany's New Era 33

The Reagan Revolution and Social Security 39

"Red" and Gray 55

Mario Cuomo and the Family of New York 63

Albany in the Cuomo Years 73

An EPIC Battle: The Fight for Prescription
Drug Coverage in New York 79

Greedy Geezers, Greedy Doctors
and Patients Rights 103

Recession, Deficits, Budget Cuts 121

Transition: Changing New York 133

Withering on the Vine: Fighting the
Gingrich Revolution 145

On the March Again: Fighting HMOs
and Drug Companies 153

Goodbye Rose 157

On Others Shoulders: Carrying on the Legacy . . . 165

"Maple Power: Peace, Love,
and Cheap Drugs" 171

Epilogue 181

Council Board Members 185

FOREWORD

THIS IS A BOOK ABOUT A DECADES-LONG MOVEMENT OF OLDER Americans to fight for improvements in the quality of life for themselves and their peers. It is a story of how they fought for all the major changes and programs in American society which have resulted in such a grand reversal of the plight of the elderly in the second half of the twentieth century, changes that have led to an increased lifespan, less poverty and a better quality of life. It is a story of a generation of older people who grew up in the early part of the twentieth century in New York City and New York State and who, in their youth, were committed to progressive causes including social insurance and social equity. They supported the efforts of New York Governor and later President Franklin D. Roosevelt to lift many out of poverty through Social Security and other landmark pieces of legislation in the New Deal.

This is also a story that focuses on the life of one of those activists, Rose Kryzak of Queens, a Russian immigrant whose life spanned the entire twentieth century before she passed away in its final year. She was active in social causes throughout her life but became most noted when she retired and became a senior advocate a champion of her peers, especially those who were poor. It is a story of her years of activism in New York when she became such a symbol of older people's causes that she was embraced by political leaders in the city and state who admired her indefatigable spirit and her social conscience. This book is also a story about the senior citizens organizations and activists who Rose worked with over the years that provided organized means to pursue social and legislative changes that improved the lives of older New Yorkers.

Rose Kryzak was not the only senior leader or the most prominent one of her time. She had only limited national exposure and leadership roles though her successes in New York had national implications. Maggie Kuhn who founded the Gray Panthers was the best known national leader.

In other states, there were many leaders as well like the "Condo Commandos" in south Florida and leaders in state associations. But, Rose Kryzak was unique because of her humor, her feistiness, her fearlessness, her courage and, most of all, because of her background and life experiences.

She was born in czarist Russia, survived a pogrom, emigrated at Ellis Island and then became a devoted Communist activist who worked for socialism in the United States. She later endured the McCarthy era when her brother, who was a leader in the Communist Party, went underground and was sought by the FBI. She helped the Rosenberg children be adopted after their parents were executed as spies, and she even opened her door to serve lunch to Martin Luther King, Jr. when her neighbor's daughter brought him home during their college years. All of that happened before Rose retired and became a senior activist. Though her roots were not in the labor movement, she saw life through the working class eye. Her activism was based on poverty not just social theory.

This book seeks to remind readers that the programs and benefits which were passed into law didn't just happen by chance. They were the result of advocacy actions by Rose Kryzak and others. In some cases, like the passage of New York State's EPIC prescription drug coverage program, it simply wouldn't have happened if Rose and her peers didn't take action. It took courage and a determined effort by Rose, other senior advocates and organizations to literally snatch victory from what had been proclaimed a dead issue by the then-Governor of New York, Mario Cuomo. It is a reminder that yes, in our democracy, the people still do have power when they use it.

Despite the big difference in our ages, Rose Kryzak became a great friend of mine after I became Executive Director of the New York StateWide Senior Action Council in 1982. She was like another grandmother to me. I invited her to visit with my mother and later, after I got married, with my wife and children. We went on vacation together in the Adirondacks. Over the nearly two decades of our friendship, I had many conversations with her, wrote some of her anecdotes and funny stories in my diary, and in her last years, I videotaped and recorded her oral account of many of the events of her life. Those tapes and writings are the basis of many parts of this book along with the newsletters and archives of the New York StateWide Senior Action Council, public documents and newspaper articles. Carol Wallace who worked for StateWide in the 1990s and loved Rose interviewed her for several hours and those audio tapes of Rose's oral history are included.

In that this book discusses the battle on issues and for social changes over a few decades, it is also a story about New York State politics and its leaders over the last quarter of the twentieth century. From our office a block from the New York State Capitol, we have had an influence on important legislation and seen how politics and personalities influenced those victories. Rose's special relationship with former Governor Mario Cuomo, who served during half of those years, is an important part of this story. Rose also interacted with the other men and women who were leaders in the New York State Legislature during those years. And, she was a guest on local and national media programs including ABC's *Good*

Morning America and *Nightline* programs. Above all, this is a story of the heroes who worked to change the face of American life for older persons and their families. And, it is a call to action for readers of all ages about just how important it is to participate in our democratic process to advocate for important social changes.

CHAPTER ONE

THE BIRTH OF THE SENIOR ACTION MOVEMENT

IN THE COURSE OF JUST ONE GENERATION, THE PUBLIC PERCEPTION OF older Americans was transformed by a group of activists from one of self-reliant, under-educated, poor and silent suffering to one of a powerful political constituency able to influence public policy in Washington, D.C. and state capitals across the country. Like other interest groups in the second half of the twentieth century, seniors organized a movement and demanded action to address serious problems of poverty, lack of access to adequate health care and many other issues they uniquely faced.

"Senior power" was an oxymoron in the middle of the twentieth century as new senior citizens' organizations were born. At the time, older persons were viewed as being independent and self-reliant and not interested in promoting their needs. They didn't think in terms of their own "needs," because they had lived with the ethic of self-reliance. Seeking government assistance for any need was an admission of failure. Most were too proud to seek it. Growing up through the years of the Great Depression, they learned to survive and to make do economically. Many of the older persons of that era were also foreign-born and they did not easily relate to

American political participation other than voting.

As Dr. Robert N. Butler wrote at the beginning of his influential 1975 book, *Why Survive? Being Old in America:*

"Old age in America is often a tragedy. Few of us like to consider it because it reminds us of our own mortality. It demands our energy and resources, it frightens us with illness and deformity, it is an affront to a culture with a passion for youth and productive capacity. We are so pre-occupied with defending ourselves from the reality of death that we ignore the fact that human beings are alive until they are actually dead."

Seniors were not viewed as "powerful" in any public way. There were viewed as kind and wise family figures, but there were also many negative stereotypes of older persons in society as senile "geezers," of limited education, or old women with squeaky high voices who were somewhat infantile and dependent and who danced the "hokey pokey." Television shows like *I Love Lucy* showed Ricky and Lucy trying to scare away two young people with crushes on them by dressing up as hard-of-hearing invalids with Ricky needing his legs shaken to improve his circulation.

A late-1970's study by the University of Pennsylvania's Annenberg School of Communications confirmed all this. The study concluded that old men were often found in TV dramas to possess powers that are evil and punished by death. Older women were likely to be victimized by all groups of dramatic characters. The more TV viewers watched, the more they believed that people - especially women - reached old age earlier in life than they actually do. In a 1979 article in *Senior Action*, the newspaper of the StateWide Senior Action Council, the writer asked,

"Why is it harmful to be depicted in an erroneous way on TV or any other medium? Precisely because others tend to treat us as they perceive us. And if seniors are made to look like eccentrics or weak-willed creatures, who let themselves be walked all over the minute they turn 60, then, you can be certain that certain groups of people as well as individuals may try to take advantage. Some that come instantly to mind are unscrupulous businessmen, advertisers and others who stand to benefit in economic areas. Then government on every level has a tendency to play Big Brother if not God. And finally there are those relatives who think domination is the only way to show concern."

It wasn't until the Golden Girls hit television in the 1980's that a newer view of seniors emerged.

Older Americans did have problems and a movement began to improve their quality of life in both economic and social ways. Half of older persons did not have health insurance of any kind before Medicare. There were no coordinated senior services to provide meal programs, no transportation services for isolated seniors, no special housing for seniors living alone in large houses. There were private programs like the first Senior Center in the country, which was established in New York City in the late 1940's and run by Gertrude Landau. However, the plight of older persons - with over a third living in poverty - touched the conscience of many as America became a more affluent nation.

The birth of the senior citizens' movement can be traced back to the Townsend Movement in the 1930's which was an active campaign in California to gain pensions. There were Townsend Clubs established across the country to promote the idea. Later, the AARP (American Association of Retired Persons) was founded in 1958 by Dr. Ethel Percy Andrus as an outgrowth of the National

Retired Teachers Association (NRTA) which she had founded in 1947. The AARP became a retiree organization for those who weren't teachers and offered health insurance and benefits to its members.

The birth of the modern, grassroots activist senior movement can be traced to 1961 when the National Council of Senior Citizens was formed by the AFL-CIO following the White House Conference on the Aging that year. The National Council pushed hard for the passage of Medicare in the 1960's. Later in the decade, Maggie Kuhn, formed the Gray Panthers, an organization of seniors but one that fought for a whole range of social justice issues for all ages. Kuhn became the most well-known and acclaimed senior activist in the country as she sought a cultural revolution to change the role and view of older Americans. She was also outspoken in opposing the Vietnam War. She sought to build an activist army of older people to fight for their own rights but also to fight for other progressive policies. She said:

"I am very concerned about the fact that so many of my peers do not have a goal. You retire from a job and retire from life...the rocking chair and leisure world. What a waste!...We who have no risk to fear, we who have historical perspective, we who can take the challenge of change, ought to be leading the charge, ought to be out of the rocking chairs."

While the senior movement was building in its early years, the fight for a national health insurance program like Medicare had been going on for decades. In fact, the original Social Security bill included health coverage but President Roosevelt dropped it, fearing it might doom the Social Security bill altogether. President Truman made an effort to enact national health insurance but he failed.

Serious efforts to pass a medical program took root during President Kennedy's term.

The long battle for some form of national health insurance for older Americans was finally won with the passage of Medicare in 1965 during a flurry of social legislation pushed by President Lyndon Johnson after President Kennedy was assassinated. Also passed at that time was the Older Americans Act. This act was most significant in building the senior movement because it established the Administration on Aging that institutionalized funding for an infrastructure of senior centers and county offices for the aging. They were funded to provide many new aging services including meals programs, legal services for the elderly, senior employment programs and other services. Each county agency also had to have an advisory committee of seniors. This on-going funding built a constituency of provider agencies and the seniors who actively participated in their activities and programs.

In 1961, the first White House Conference on the Aging had been held and recommendations from it led to the advocacy effort that resulted in the passage of Medicare and the Older Americans Act. A second White House Conference was held in 1971. Following that event, Congress continued to improve and expand senior programs. In 1972, Congress passed legislation establishing the Supplemental Security Income (SSI) program which provided a supplement to Social Security for the very poor, aged, blind and disabled whose Social Security checks were well below the poverty level. The program began on January 1, 1974. Annual cost of living adjustments (COLAs) were enacted for both Social Security and SSI.

In New York State in 1961, Governor Nelson Rockefeller established a Division of the Aging in the Department of Social Welfare. The current New York State Office for the Aging was created as an independent agency in 1965. The senior action movement in

New York State was born in 1972 with the formation of the New York StateWide Senior Action Council. It was formed in response to recommendations of the 1971 White House Conference on Aging to create vehicles for seniors to have a voice to advocate for themselves. StateWide would be a grassroots organization that also had its roots in Lyndon Johnson's War on Poverty. StateWide was formed at a time when money was flowing from Washington, D.C. not just for services but for advocacy, to empower the poor to have a voice in designing programs and policies to improve their lives. A committee of community action agency staff began meeting in 1970, the organizational meeting was held in Glens Falls in 1972 and the New York StateWide Senior Action Council was incorporated.

Robert O'Donnell became the first director of the organization in 1973 and set up its main office in New York City with other offices in Rochester and later in Syracuse and Albany. He became a legend with senior activists in those years because he displayed a fierce loyalty to them and great compassion. As an ex-priest, he tended to the seniors like they were members of his parish. He was concerned about their personal problems and always had time to talk.

He was a flamboyant advocate and teacher too. He was famous for his dramatic rhetoric. "We are no longer buying the image that we are sitting at home in rocking chairs waiting to die." Many seniors always remembered his preaching about P-O-W-E-R, how he used each letter to explain one of the features of the word and how seniors had to use their power.

P stands for people. Many think of power as money - you buy it. Seniors don't have money, but they have numbers. They are the fastest growing minority in the country. In New York State, they comprise 22 percent of the total number of registered voters.

O means organize and form coalitions. "Get out of your centers, work with the young and the disabled."

W stands for work. Power doesn't come to those who sit back and wait. You must work to organize power."

E is for education. Old dogs can't learn new tricks is a lie. Educate yourselves and then educate the general public. Find out what's in the Older Americans Act and other pieces of legislation.

R will mean results. National conferences on the aging discuss the same issues year after year. Don't let the professionals always speak for you. Speak out yourselves. You're only asking to be repaid for what you have given this country. Let us get back into the mainstream of American living."

StateWide's focus would be on state as well as national issues. Democrat Hugh Carey won a landslide victory in 1974, riding the waves of Watergate to oust Republican incumbent Malcolm Wilson who was elevated to the post just a year earlier when Nelson A. Rockefeller, the legend who had dominated New York State politics since 1959 decided to step down. Wilson, a decent and urbane man, was never able to establish himself in the void left by Rockefeller in that year of the Watergate scandal and a stumbling economy.

With Carey came the first activist director of the New York State Office for the Aging, Mrs. Lou Glasse. She had been a county director in Poughkeepsie, Dutchess County. She appointed Jane Gould as her legislative and constituency liaison and she and Bob O'Donnell became fast friends who would work together to push senior advocacy at the legislative and grassroots level. Governor Carey named Bob to be co-chair of the Governor's Transitional Task Force on Aging which produced a report with recommendations resulting from its activities in the first six months of 1975.

The 1970's were the decade when senior power became not only a rising phenomenon but also was impressed in the consciousness of those who were active. StateWide was an unlikely organization of unique composition. Indeed, the fact that it was originally a creation of anti-poverty funding meant that people who would not normally join together did. There were poor and middle class whites from small rural counties getting together with some of the poorest older African-Americans from Harlem and the inner cities of Rochester and Buffalo, many of whom had migrated decades earlier from the Deep South.

This membership made StateWide unlike other senior organizations. The AARP was the best known organization for older persons with millions of members nationwide and in the state. Many were professional and educated persons of middle and upper-middle incomes. The AARP however did not establish any state legislative offices to make it more effective at the local level. It wasn't until the mid-1990's that such an office was set up in Albany. The National Council of Senior Citizens had a state chapter of union retirees whose leaders like Albert Blumberg and Eleanor Litwak worked closely with StateWide in the following years. Their background in organized labor gave them a different focus but they maintained their union traditions of activism.

There were also many local advocacy organizations in New York City. In the coming years, StateWide would work closely with Dan Sambol and Delissa James of the Federation of Protestant Welfare Agencies, Suleika Cabrera Drinane of the Hispanic Senior Action Council, the Coalition of Concerned for Older Americans

(COCOA) led by Leora Magier, and Judi Duhl, Caryn Resnick and later Marjorie Lipkin and Amy West Poley of the Joint Public Affairs Committee (JPAC) of the Jewish Association of Services for the Aged. In later years the Brooklynwide Interagency Council on the Aging headed by Shirley Genn would become very public in its advocacy among the boroughwide councils. Andrew Koski of the Brookdale Center on Aging worked with StateWide on public policy and benefits issues. In the 1980's Citywide Advocates for Seniors played a major role in coordinated state level advocacy efforts among New York City senior centers and clubs.

So, StateWide wasn't the only senior organization that was an active advocacy organization, but it was the only one trying to coordinate this activism among all seniors across the state. StateWide was an organization of persons involved in senior citizen centers and senior clubs and those involved in low income programs through county offices for the aging and community action agencies that were created with the War on Poverty.

StateWide became especially strong in some inner-city minority communities in Rochester, Buffalo and New York City. And, in rural areas, like the North Country along the Canadian border, the organization got strong support from leaders of the county offices for the aging like Joe Sears in St. Lawrence County and Bob O'Connell in Rensselaer County. They had attended StateWide's organizational meeting. While many in the rural areas had not been activists like urban members who might have been in unions, the rural seniors were joiners, always willing to participate in a community event or petition drive to help StateWide.

While StateWide did not have its own financial and institutional base like the other senior groups, it did emerge in the 1970's as the most effective senior force across the state because of the sheer will and enthusiasm of its members.

StateWide's presence did not go unnoticed and led to controversy and competition in its early years. Nelson Cruickshank, President of the National Council of Senior Citizens, protested to the Administration on Aging that the State Office for the Aging was encouraging county agencies to use federal funds to finance seniors' expenses to take part in StateWide's meetings. Bob O'Donnell saw that as an attempt to undermine the organization even though StateWide had reached out to the National Council's state chapter to cooperate on a number of fronts.

The vast majority of older persons were not involved with any senior organizations. They were more likely to be involved with the American Legion, their own church or a civic association. However, groups like StateWide became a vehicle and a voice that articulated the concerns of older persons as a group and their influence spread to other seniors because they often were able to make news and focus public attention on key issues like health care, Social Security and the cost of energy. In fact, right from the start in its early years, StateWide would be continually focused on concerns about income security and health care that would be the centerpiece of its work for the next three decades.

As the 1970's began, much of the focus of aging advocacy was on the poverty rates among older Americans. In the early 1970's, one of every four older Americans still had incomes below the federal poverty level. At that time, as Dr. Butler noted, "Poverty or drastically lowered income and old age go hand in hand." President Jimmy Carter would call elderly poverty, "a national disgrace." In its early years StateWide would focus on the implementation of the SSI program (Supplemental Security Income) to supplement the income of poor Social Security recipients. StateWide helped establish a State Temporary Committee to Monitor SSI. Bob O'Donnell also testified on the problems of SSI before the US Senate

Special Committee on Aging chaired by Senator Frank Church of Idaho.

Universal health care was a clarion call for StateWide then and now as senior activists wanted to complete the dream of social insurance that Social Security and Medicare had only partly fulfilled. At the 1971 White House Conference on the Aging, a resolution was passed calling for prescription drug coverage under Medicare and the issue would become a signature one for StateWide. The issue would be a prime focus of StateWide's advocacy throughout its history. From its early years, StateWide pushed for "a national health security program including comprehensive long-term and in-home services for the elderly."

StateWide also gave a vehicle to those persons who were activists, mostly liberals who in their younger years worked for social justice whether in the Civil Rights Movement or the union movement. Several had been active in the Communist Party in their younger years. StateWide organized its members and there were many such activists in the leadership. Its staff and leaders traveled across the state and helped local senior groups to organize county councils of senior citizens in 35 of the state's 62 counties.

Carl Eberhart of Clayton on the St. Lawrence River became StateWide's second president in 1974. He was very active in a number of community organizations and brought that energy and experience to StateWide. He exhorted his colleagues to build the organization.

As president of StateWide, I am one of three million senior citizens over 60 in New York State. Alone I can do nothing. With your help there is nothing we can't do. Our name is StateWide Senior ACTION Council. Let's have the action. Do you have friends whose motto is "Never do today what you put off til tomor-

row?" Or do they say, 'I'll never live to see it?' Let's think and act positively.

First: Appoint social action committees in all local clubs, all county councils, all regions. Second: Pick your priorities. Is transportation a problem in your community? Or is it SSI, health, housing,, income?

Third: Know your legislators, whether village, town, school or state. Remind them that 75 to 85 percent of senior citizens vote. They're not stupid.

If we can be of assistance, ask. We are not infallible but we'll try. No request will be ignored. Let's make StateWide the most powerful group in the state. We can do it."

StateWide set up its main office in New York City with a satellite office in Rochester. By the end of the 1970's, StateWide had other offices in Albany and Syracuse as well. StateWide published a newspaper, *Senior Action*, that was distributed free to about 30,000 older persons and organizations in the state. Every year, the organization had an annual convention, usually held at the Hotel Syracuse. At these conventions, priority issues for advocacy were discussed and agreed upon.

Following incorporation and initial funding in 1973, board members had been recruited. Many seniors who attended the organizational meeting in 1972 became active on the board. In New York City, a short little woman, Rose Kryzak was retiring at age 73 after spending 52 years working at the actuarial firm, Buck Associates:

"Because I had retired in 1972 and I was getting adjusted to retirement, and in 1973 I was looking, I realized I needed something to do but I knew I had to do something with people. I went

into a (senior) center and the director said, 'What do you like to do'? I said, 'I don't know but what I do know is: it has to do with people. I would like to be something like in political action or public affairs.' He said, 'Well, you are the chair of the political action (committee), which I did. And that is how it all started, so it was in '73 that I became active in the senior citizen movement."

CHAPTER TWO

ROSE KRYZAK — BORN WITH THE CENTURY

Russia in the Time of the Czars

ORN JUST TWO AND HALF MONTHS BEFORE THE TWENTIETH century dawned, Rose Kryzak would lead a life that would intersect with American history in the new century. She was born on October 15, 1899 into a Jewish family in Minsk in today's Belarus under the czar. Hers was a life of bitter poverty and prejudice so great that she always remembered the Christians celebrating Easter with a pogrom in her village, smashing windows in her house and many others. She grew up always disliking Easter.

Her father came to America in 1907 and worked. By 1910, she was on a boat, arriving at Ellis Island in New York Harbor. She went to school and then to work. But her childhood in Russia was filled with painful memories:

"We lived in a house where everybody lived together. My grandfather, I only remember him as doing nothing but always combing his beard. My grandmother ran the laundry, she did all the work, he only went to the synagogue every day and always looked well-groomed and very elegant. He (my grandfather) always looked very elegant to me but never did any work. And I am resentful

about that. My poor grandmother, whom I loved dearly, she worked so hard, but I didn't quite understand what was going on. Nobody could tell me, nor would I ask either. I didn't ask until I came here, until I came to America.

Well, I tell you, there wasn't anything to remember, it was so dull. Dull and dreary and not much happiness. We lived through a pogrom and my mother had asked a Christian family to take us in and he (the father) agreed and when we got there, I remember that very distinctly. When we came to his house we found that he had taken his children out to somewhere else. My mother, when she saw that he took his children out, she said to us: 'Since he took his children out, his house is no protection to us, so let's go out and stand and face the enemy.' He just betrayed my mother.

All this happened in one day, but never got beyond a certain point. They stopped before. I never saw the people who were doing the pillaging and the killing but the fright that was there. I don't know how many people were killed.

In those three years, in Russia, we lived with my grandmother. From seven to ten (years old) I remember very distinctly. They were very lean years. We had very little. It was in White Russia, the town of Minsk. My mother's name was Anne. I don't know what my grandmother's English name, Rissa, would be. Rubens, that was my mother's maiden name. My maiden name was Marron.

Ellis Island and Coming to America

"My mother would tell us that someday my father would send for us but the next thing I knew he came, he was there, he came from America, but the story is that there was a big depression in 1907. The reason why I remember there was a depression in 1907 was that my father came back from America. See, he was here (United States) but somehow I don't remember when he went here

(United States) but I remember…my mother saying that someday we would all be here.

Whatever money he had saved up he couldn't get it out. He was a house painter and he couldn't get it and he decided to come back to Russia and see if he could make something there but things were bad there too, so then he decided to go back to America and then we had to wait three years til he sent for us and we came to America in 1910.

Ellis Island is a story I have to tell. I was 10 years old. In Russia we got on the boat. My father sent us the money … We got on a boat and I don't remember the city but I know it took us 18 days to get to New York, on the steerage. It was awful. We didn't like the food and we slept on big - you know like layers- bunk beds. They were at least two high and we were on the top, so that at least was good. It was hot and we were hungry but the only thing we liked that they gave us was this white, gummy bread and we never had white bread in Russia, so we thought it was wonderful to have white bread like when you were sick. We used to get white bread in Russia but here we got it every day. The 18 days were so endless and we never ate anything but milk and white bread. They used to bring the food in trash cans. They were clean because I remember I know now what a trash can looks like but they had to bring a lot because there were a lot of immigrants. I didn't like it, I used to say they smelled bad. Anyway, we survived.

Then we arrived at Ellis Island and the night before we arrived there, I've never forgot, my mother practically scalped me and my sister. No, not shaved, scrubbed because maybe they would find lice on our heads and my mother said if they find any lice they may send us back.

School Days

I didn't go to school (in Russia). No, I didn't read, I didn't write. We had no books. I don't remember books in my life. The funny thing is when I came to this country and I went to PS 150 at 96th St. and First Avenue between First and Second Avenue and if I got a B plus my father would say 'What happened?' He expected A's, all A's and I'd be afraid to come home if I ever got a B plus which wasn't very often. When I went to school, he had to sign my report card."

Rose finished the eighth grade and graduated at the age of 15. Her mother said she couldn't go to high school because they couldn't afford it. "I was heartbroken, but I accepted it." She got a job in a feather factory earning $4 a week. Her mother gave her lunch and carfare. Rose took the Lexington Avenue trolley to 34th Street. The factory was opposite Gimbels Department Store. One side was feathers. The 32nd Street side was flowers.

Her boss asked Rose to deliver Christmas presents. Rose got tips, especially from important people like Victor Herbert whom she loved. One hundred people worked in the factory. Rose's job was to sort feathers and she found it very boring.

Meanwhile, she finally was able to go to Wadley High School at night for free at 114th Street near Columbus Avenue. She took an academic course of liberal arts for about a year and a half. She got to do everything and she learned the Dewey Decimal System. Then, her mother got sick and Rose had to take care of three other siblings.

Her father was very poor, earning just $13 a week to support a family of five. He was a housepainter, but he was a very cultured person who took the family to free concerts at the Met on Friday nights. The kids sat on the floor to listen as he talked about the plight of workers. He was frustrated that he was not an American or a trained worker and had no hope to rise through the ranks. He took Rose to meetings where the talk was about social security and pensions. No one else talked about it. Her father always said, "You see someone in need, be sure to help." He was a very compassionate person.

Her mother wanted her father to make more money, but he said, "All I have is my hands to sell." When it snowed, the city would pay $2 a night for men to shovel. Her mother died at the age of 58 and her father re-married. Rose was grateful. They were married 11 years, then her step-mother died. Her father lived with Rose and her husband for the last few years of his life.

Eventually Rose got a job in Buck Associates, an actuarial firm, in 1920. With the exception of a few years when her children were born, Rose would remain there for 52 years. It was at Buck Associates that she had her first experience as an advocate. She loved her job, getting paid 48 cents an hour. The company gave holidays off, but they were not paid. She finally decided to ask the boss why the workers weren't being paid for twelve holidays as promised. She complained to her supervisor. Then, she was called in by the boss. Mr. Buck called a staff meeting and egged Rose on. He went through the issue and Rose challenged him politely. An hour later he sent for Rose. Everyone including Rose was worried that she was going to lose her job. However, Mr. Buck said he liked her because she stuck to her guns. He gave her a raise and instituted paid holidays. After that, she became the spokesperson for the workers. "It gave me courage," she would later say.

In 1923, she was rowing on a lake in New York when she heard a man in a nearby canoe speaking Russian. Rose said hello in Russian. The man invited her into his canoe. She went and "I never got out," she would say. George Kryzak, whom she called Kay, took her out to dinner later that week. He sent her a big box of flowers on her birthday and took her to see *Rigoletto*. She married George the next year and they would be together for 62 years.

Rose's sister married George's brother and the children of both couples would be very close. Her sister's two daughters, Lucy and Barbara, considered Rose and George as surrogate parents, especially in later years after their own parents died.

George was studying to be a pharmacist at Union College in Schenectady. Before they met, Rose had planned to travel across the country. She offered to give up the trip because she was in love with George, but he encouraged her to go. She warned him she would be gone a long time and would have to earn some money along the way. He promised to have $300 waiting in California. She worked in Chicago on the way out. Then, she was in Walla Walla, Washington and picked fruit. She stayed at a migrant camp in Oregon where she picked hops and she made a lot of friends there. She went on and stayed at the YWCA in San Francisco. She met two girls from Chicago who begged her to join them on the return trip. One hundred miles east of Los Angeles, they ran out of highway so they decided to jump a train! They flagged one down and they rode on top all the way to the Grand Canyon. They saw many hobos who rode the rails and who were warned by the conductor to stay away from the girls. George was so glad to see Rose when she got back east and then they got married.

CHAPTER THREE

HEAT OR EAT: THE ENERGY CRISIS AND OLDER NEW YORKERS IN THE 1970S

IN THE EARLY 1970'S, ENERGY ISSUES BECAME A MAJOR FOCUS OF national attention. The 1973 war in the Middle East spawned global economic chaos and recession. The Arab oil boycott had driven the cost of energy up from its historically low prices. High energy prices were a particular concern for older Americans living on fixed incomes.

The life and death threat of energy costs was dramatized by a tragedy on Christmas Eve 1973 in Schenectady that received national attention. Two seniors in their nineties, Frank and Catherine Baker, froze to death in their home after Niagara Mohawk had disconnected their gas service. Their deaths created an uproar in the community, with people wondering how such a thing could happen especially during the holiday season. The Bakers' deaths led to major changes in utility policies at the state level. Subsequent investigations would reveal that the couple had money in the bank to pay their utility bill, but their deaths showed that operating a utility company without regard to the life-threatening consequences of disconnection of service in the winter led to the tragedy.

Reeling from the very human tragedy of the Bakers' deaths,

the utilities and the Public Service Commission moved to establish "demonstration projects" in Monroe and Schenectady counties, instituting protective services for persons who might not be able to handle their own affairs. Many people though began to call for an outright ban on utility terminations during winter months. The state Public Service Commission did decide to prevent the recurrence of any holiday tragedies by ordering the suspension of terminations for the two-week period encompassing Christmas and New Year's Day. However, the Commission sided with the utilities and felt the threat of termination was an effective inducement for payment and it refused to approve the outright winter ban.

The public pressure continued to mount and by 1977, four years after the Bakers deaths, the Commission did pass new regulations declaring November 1 to April 15 of each year to be a cold weather period. The regulations were an expanded version of the protective services demonstration projects and they required utility companies to make personal contact before terminating service at any household and to refer persons defined as having hardships to a local social services agency. The companies had to change their whole approach to customer service. After years of saying they weren't a social services agency, they found out they had to incorporate some features of them.

Advocates kept pushing for more consumer protections and customer rights that would be clearly defined in law. Assemblyman Oliver Koppell and Senator Joseph Pisani sponsored a bill, dubbed the "utility consumers bill of rights" which passed the Assembly but which was bottled up by the utilities in the Senate. In 1981, Governor Carey finally threw his weight behind it and the tide turned. The utilities decided they would have to negotiate a compromise. In July 1981, Carey signed the Home Energy Fair Practices Act, the first utility bill of rights in the nation. It established and expanded a series of protections including those which further restricted terminations, placed limits on estimated billings, virtually eliminated security deposits and suspended terminations for medical emergencies. Consumer and senior groups working together proved they could change public policy in New York.

Thoughout the 1970's, Niagara Mohawk and other utilities asked for huge rate increases every year, triggering widespread community protests. In the winter of 1976, hundreds of people showed up at hearings across upstate New York to protest.

The rising cost of energy also led to growing calls for municipal governments to take control of the utilities and establish public power just like the water service run by most municipalities. The village of Massena in northern New York on the Canadian border is the site of the St. Lawrence Seaway and power project. Local residents wondered why they couldn't benefit from the state power project in their own town. Led by activists from the United Auto Workers at the local Chevrolet plant, the Town Board voted to hold a referendum on public power in 1974 to take over Niagara Mohawk Power Corporation and run their own local utility like over 40 other municipalities in the state. The vote led to a bitter community battle with Niagara Mohawk dispatching workers door to door to urge defeat of the proposal. On election day, the villagers rejected the utility and voted to form their own utility service. Niagara Mohawk immediately went to court and the issue was tied up for seven years before the Massena Electric Department finally was established and offered dramatic reductions in electricity bills.

Senior citizen leaders were active in other local communities around the state trying to push for municipal power. In New York City, similar efforts were underway to expropriate Con Edison and establish a New York City power company. An organization called

POWER was formed and Rose Kryzak joined the fray. Ever since she got involved three years earlier in senior citizens' activities, she was constantly on the go. She became very active in many of these public issues involving energy including public power and rate increases. There were other more technical issues like whether the utilities should be able to charge consumers for power plants being constructed for future use. It was that issue which first catapulted Rose Kryzak to regional and national attention.

In 1976, she had heard there was going to be a hearing by the Federal Power Commission in New York City. The subject was CWIP, as it was known in the regulatory circles, "construction work in progress." Rose went into the hearing and observed a formal proceeding at which several witnesses in business suits from utility companies were making their case for including these costs in the utility rates. Rose recalled:

"In 1976, I was in the field of aging only three years at that period where energy costs were very high. It was very hot and people were struggling with their energy bills. I would organize campaigns to investigate why is it that we in New York were paying so much more for a kilowatt hour than any other city in the country and I found out that there were a lot of phantom taxes and I really made a big study of it. One day I saw a little notice in the (New York) Times that the Federal Public Service Commission (Federal Power Commission) was coming to New York...That's interesting, maybe I can learn something different or more. So I went down to 26 Federal Plaza, which was where the federal government had their hearings and when I got there, (it) was a room filled with very impressive (people) mostly men. There was hardly a seat but I finally found a seat and I heard a pipeline company say, 'If you will give us $20 million dollars we will build facilities that in 20

years people will have tremendous improvements in living and the quality of life will greatly be improved'. I realized, I was then 76 years old and I said, in 20 years, I will be 96 years old and if I am alive I wonder if I will even know how to use those great improvements they are offering. I better get up and say something. So I asked the clerk that goes around to give whatever, water, I give him a note that I want to speak for 5 minutes (and for him to) send the note to the commissioners; there were three of them at the table. The clerk comes back to tell me to come out in the hall and to tell me that it was not possible; all the time had been allocated. Every company who got 20 minutes for its president, its banker and lawyer. I said, 'I want you to go back and say I think that each company can say in 19 minutes what they can say in 20 minutes and give me one minute of that time. I only want 5 minutes'.

He told me he doesn't think it is possible. I say, 'Listen young man, you don't have to go, I'll go up myself.' He got very nervous about that. He didn't want me to go up there. So he went up with my message and he came back and told me that I could have 5 minutes at 12:00. It was at that time 11:00 and I didn't really think I would get the time but I had one hour and I figured out what to say. I said that senior citizens were now having a hard time to pay for their bills and many of them may not live to enjoy all the promised goodies and should not have to pay for something they would not get to enjoy. And I left."

Rose's remarks caused such a stir that the next day, *The New York Times* reported what happened and coined the industry phrase "the Kryzak problem" in a major article in the business section. The problem was whether older people should be asked to pay through their current rates the cost of facilities that wouldn't be producing power for many years. Rose was later contacted:

In October of that year, I got a call from Washington that I won a great big victory. I wasn't home, but the call came from Washington and my husband took a message and he asked them what I had won; they said I should read the New York Times and the next day, in the business section appeared this article:

"In a homespun rebuttal to the sophisticated arguments of Wall Street banks and utility lawyers, Mrs. Kryzak said she spoke for 22 million senior citizens, including two million in New York State. Many, she said, lacked "adequate income in retirement." The Government should not let utilities charge consumers for facilities not yet producing power, Mrs. Kryzak contended. "We cannot afford plants that most of us would not live to enjoy," she said. "I am 75 years old and do you think that any pipeline or any plant is going to benefit me?" At the commission, the problem of charging today's customers for tomorrow's power, a so-called economic transfer between age generations, also became known as 'the Kryzak problem."

The utilities received only a small fraction of the financial relief they had sought for construction work in progress, only allowing charges for equipment pollution control and to convert from oil to natural gas. Rose loved going up against corporate giants. In the following years, as a Board member of StateWide she took the lead in fighting the oil companies who had become villains for high prices and were convicted of massive overcharges.

The FPC testimony and subsequent victory marked the first time Rose Kryzak had come to regional or national attention and it marked the beginning of her legendary status in the senior community. The media had pounced on the paradox of seeing a little older woman break into a regulatory hearing of briefcases and technical language and use "homespun" plain talk from a consumer's perspective. She looked and acted like a loving grandmother and she had a disarming sense of humor that made even those who were her targets like her. She was just 4' 10" but she would say later to an interviewer:

"You know the term, 'She's ten feet tall?' I feel so sure of what I have to say when I get up to speak; I feel like I'm a big, big person. I don't know whether it's immodest or what. I never think of myself as being a little nothing. I think of myself as a big, big something."

That was Rose's power and her "performance" that day and in other events led to requests for her to represent seniors on television. After the Federal Power Commission decision was announced, she appeared on ABC's *Good Morning America* to discuss her "victory."

A few years later, in the spring of 1979, with inflation raging in double digits, she was back on the show in a week-long segment on inflation with Alfred Kahn, appointed by President Carter to be his "czar" to fight it. A few consumers from around the country were invited to participate from the White House with Kahn for the daily discussions. Noting her appearances, the New York Daily News wrote a feature about Rose, "the biggest problem in getting a story from 78-year-old Rose Kryzak about herself and her many volunteer activities as 'an advocate for senior citizens' is to catch up with her."

Rose loved the senior advocacy movement. She was a real advocate, a doer who was always ready to take part in every organizing event. "To be old and to be around is very nice, but the trick is to be old and to be well," she would tell an interviewer years later.

Despite her advancing years, she remained in good health. She was ready to be the leader or spokesperson though she was not power hungry. She never sought titles. She had confidence in her ability to speak and to have an impact. She didn't need a title. Like many of the seniors who had grown up as socialists or Communists during the Great Depression, she always had her "eyes on the prize." She wasn't interested in negotiating piecemeal compromises on the issues. She wanted public power and national health care and she wasn't impressed with gradual steps to those goals because she believed they were the real solutions. She even got impatient discussing minor improvements.

She and others were adamant in rejecting the slightest cuts or changes in existing programs which was understandable. However, as the federal budget deficits began to soar in the 1980's and there were calls for cuts or changes in Social Security, she would have no part of it. For example, many of the New Deal generation were outraged at any suggestion to re-figure or cut the annual cost of living adjustment in Social Security. Pragmatists often felt it was better to give a little on the edges than to let opponents destroy the program. Rose felt advocates should never endorse cuts. If they came to be, she didn't want her fingerprints on the deal.

And, she always saw the bigger picture and tried to talk about it wherever she went. At a February 1978 conference at the World Trade Center on crime prevention and victim assistance programs for senior citizens in New York City, Rose told the *Daily News* that "criminals are not just the youth who prey on the elderly but also the unscrupulous landlords, doctors and public utilities who take advantage of them."

CHAPTER FOUR

ALBANY'S NEW ERA

B Y THE END OF THE 1970'S, STATE GOVERNMENT AND THE CITY of Albany itself had dramatically changed. As the decade began, Governor Nelson Rockefeller had been all powerful controlling state business and the budget with his staff resources. The Legislature began the decade with small offices crammed into the Capitol Building. By the end of the decade they had their own offices in a new marble Legislative Office Building that was part of the monstrous Empire State Plaza that Rockefeller had envisioned and then fought for that took over a decade to build.

The story goes that Governor Rockefeller was so embarrassed by the old city of Albany when Holland's Princess Beatrix came in 1959 to visit Dutch roots in America that he began planning a dazzling transformation to make the city worthy of its visitors and him.

The project displaced 9,000 people in the working class brownstones in the blocks adjacent to the Capitol. In its place, Rockefeller's dream became a futuristic, Oz-like skyline of four 20 story marble towers, a 44-story larger tower, a spaceship or football shaped Performing Arts Center the locals would dub, "The Egg" and a Cultural Education Center to include the State Museum and Library. Underground, it was all connected by a long concourse and three levels of parking garages. Above ground, a new skating rink and reflecting pool with black-dyed water spanned its length. It was into this vast complex of buildings that seniors and citizen activists would try to navigate more and more in the years ahead as they came to seek legislative action in Albany.

Dedicated as the Nelson A. Rockefeller Empire State Plaza in 1978 with the former Governor on hand to enjoy the tribute, it became either an architectural masterpiece or monstrosity depending on the viewer's opinion. A PBS show on architecture had singled it out comparing it to fascist architecture in Germany and Italy that had been built to glorify state power.

So, the Albany of 1979 was a different place when the residents of the city and state woke up to the banner headlines that this dominating millionaire ex-governor who had influenced state and national politics had died of a heart attack overnight. His era and life were now part of the history and folklore of the city and state.

A year earlier, the incumbent Governor Hugh Carey was in a tough battle with his own Lieutenant Governor, Mary Ann Krupsak, the state's first female Lieutenant Governor, challenging him in the primary. Krupsak was so annoyed that Carey neglected her and gave her little responsibility that she started the mutiny that ended her political ascendancy when Carey defeated her in the primary. Carey replaced her on the ticket by selecting Secretary of State Mario Cuomo as his running mate. Carey opted for Cuomo even though he had snubbed his own Secretary of State in favor of Ed Koch in the New York City mayoral race a year earlier in 1977. Carey would then face Assembly Minority Leader Perry Duryea in the general election.

Even though he was the incumbent, Carey wasn't highly popular and he trailed Duryea in the polls. Cuomo campaigned, and while noting that Carey wasn't all that inspiring, would say you don't have to love Hugh Carey to vote for him. Carey made a stop at

StateWide's 1978 convention in October in Syracuse. He won a come-from-behind victory for a second term and returned to Albany for his second inauguration in January 1979.

Meanwhile, the Democratic Speaker of the Assembly, Stanley Steingut of Brooklyn, was defeated in his re-election bid and when Democrats returned to Albany after the elections, they chose 44-year-old Stanley Fink of Brooklyn as their new leader. As Speaker he would hold one of the state's three most powerful jobs along with the Governor and Senate Majority Leader who was Republican Warren Anderson of Binghamton.

Fink quickly established himself as a force to be reckoned with. He made it clear he would be his own man and would not be dominated by the Democratic governor. In fact, Fink in his first year as Speaker would directly challenge Governor Hugh Carey. Many would credit Fink with making the Assembly staff more professional and able to compete with the Governor's staff and budget office rather than simply being unable to challenge their expertise. Fink also would prove to be a great ally for senior organizations like StateWide. He acknowledged that his own mother had a powerful influence on him. She would join senior groups coming to lobby him in Albany.

StateWide had adopted two primary goals for the 1979 legislative session. It continued to push for the end of mandatory retirement and it made a priority of passing a community services bill for seniors that would provide state funding for county governments to use for senior services by the local offices for the aging. Carey put this proposal in his own budget and it passed.

It was energy again, though, that came to dominate the headlines across the nation and in Albany that year and eventually led to an historic confrontation between the Legislature and Carey. StateWide played its first major role in this high profile state legislative battle in Albany. The organization had established its first office in Albany and hired staffperson Virginia Plunkett to focus on energy issues.

In the fall of 1979, prices for home heating oil were skyrocketing and many low-income and elderly persons were fearful they would not be able to pay their bills. There was debate in Albany and Washington about establishing a heating assistance program to help those in need pay so they wouldn't go without heat. StateWide's new president, Reverend Howard Hills of Valley Falls near the Vermont border, joined with Evan Pritchard of the AARP to chair the new Coalition for Action on the Home Heating Crisis, a group of seniors and energy advocates who regularly met to discuss advocacy strategies. Reverend Hills and his wife, Leora, were early builders of StateWide. After retiring from the ministry of the United Methodist Church, Reverend Hills became active in senior organizations, locally and on the advisory boards for both the Assembly and Senate Committees on Aging. Mrs. Hills became the Field Consultant for StateWide in its Capital District region in the Albany area. Reverend Hills and Leora toured the state and tried to recruit new organizations to join StateWide. They were so active in the community and at the Capitol in Albany that Reverend Hills was named Senior Citizen of the Year by the State Legislature in 1979, the first of several StateWide presidents to be given that honor.

The coalition wanted funding for heating assistance and crisis intervention. Among those involved were seniors from StateWide and other organizations like Evan Pritchard of the AARP which had a network of local seniors and chapters. Also Joyce Chupka of the Public Utility Law Project became one of the main legislative liaisons for the group. Sister Rachel Ricciardelli who worked on aging issues for Catholic Charities was never bashful about asking legislators to do something and she even went down to the Capitol in her habit to button hole them. Many joked about how she would treat them like school children and say, "Next year, we're going to do better." She made them feel like they should reply, "Yes, Sister."

The coalition pushed hard for the State Legislature to approve emergency funding for home heating for the poor. Legislators returned for a special session in late fall. The energy crisis and the cost and possible shortage of home heating oil had dominated local media in the Northeast throughout the fall. Several state legislators were drafting bills for action that would reduce the sales tax on fuel oil, create an energy assistance program on a temporary basis and provide a $35 tax credit for seniors. Reverend Hills and the group went to the third floor of the Capitol and gave legislators flyers urging action as they entered the chambers.

A special session of the State Legislature convened. Both houses of the Legislature approved the funding. Governor Hugh Carey who had entered office trying to save New York City from bankruptcy and faced serious problems with the state budget as well felt the programs were unaffordable. He signed the one reducing the sales tax on fuel oil but he vetoed the tax credit for seniors and the emergency assistance program, arguing for fiscal discipline. The vetoes set up a dramatic showdown with the Legislature.

Rarely in the history of the state were a governor's vetoes overridden, however, relations between Carey and both his own party in the Assembly and Republicans in the Senate were not close. Assembly Speaker Stanley Fink moved to override the governor's vetoes and Republican Senate Majority Leader, Warren Anderson, was only too willing to join the effort. Even though it wasn't an election year, the Legislature decided to confront the governor and scheduled votes to override the vetoes. The Senate voted 52-5 to override the Carey veto of their bill to provide heating crisis assistance to lower income households.

On November 20, 1979, the Assembly overrode the governor's veto of the heating fuel crisis assistance bill by 142-1. It was only the third time in the twentieth century that a governor's veto had been overridden. The overrides showed that when there was a popular cause or issue, legislators working with consumers and constituency groups could overwhelm even a governor who stood against them.

CHAPTER FIVE

THE REAGAN REVOLUTION
AND SOCIAL SECURITY

THE MOOD OF THE COUNTRY WAS CHANGING IN THE LATE 1970's. Proposition 13 in California which rolled back state taxes energized a whole movement which questioned the size of government and whether liberal social welfare policies had worked and whether they were sapping the nation's treasury. It was nothing new, people in upstate New York had said all that for years. But, a conservative political momentum was growing. Jimmy Carter's perceived weakness provided an easy target for the right wing and when a new round of energy prices rocked the economy in 1979 and Carter became consumed by the Iran hostage crisis in 1980, Ronald Reagan was there to pick up the pieces.

On election night, those who worked in health and human services were stunned and fearful. Advocates gathered together to decide how to fight back and limit the damage. Reagan was a man who believed in the unbridled energy of capitalism. He accused his opponents of relying on government to solve the nation's problems and that government itself was the problem.

In office, Reagan quickly proposed massive tax cuts and budget cuts. His goal as his budget director David Stockman later admitted was to starve the government of cash with such a huge tax cut

39

that there wouldn't be the ability to finance more government services. Human services advocates were appalled by Reagan's budget plan. StateWide's board was also upset and voted at its March 1981 meeting to send a letter to Reagan.

StateWide Executive Director Bob O'Donnell wrote a commentary in *Senior Action*:

"For seniors, the Reagan budget raises not only economic and political questions and problems but also and more fundamentally, serious philosophical and moral issues concerning human services. The Reagan Administration position on human services is clear. Budget Director David Stockman has stated, 'I don't think people are entitled to any services'. Martin Anderson, the president's chief domestic advisor says, 'People are quite benevolent. That's good. But is quite a different thing for people to demand that they have a right to a certain amount of income or services'.

These statements are deeply disturbing not only because they invalidate 50 years of popular and mandated social policy and development in our country but they also go against the entire Judeo-Christian concept of social justice. Both the Old and New Testament stress that a primary goal of both nation and individual is social justice for the poor. For an administration whose campaign rhetoric was so often based on the morality of issues, the importance of family and community, the role and self-independence, the concept of a "safety net" for a "truly needy" population is totally inadequate. When one seriously undermines such supportive human services for the elderly poor as minimum Social Security guarantees, food stamps, home care, senior centers, health benefits under Medicaid, housing subsidies, energy assistance, transportation subsidies, employment opportunities, nutrition programs, one also undermines the concept of self-independence versus unnec-

essary institutionalization, community and family concern versus state and community taxation and ultimately, the fundamental concept that we are a nation founded under God with principles of and a commitment to social justice for all Americans. StateWide asks you to seriously study these cutbacks in human services, pray over your deliberations, and act as if you, who have been personally responsible for the development of this country's social policy are the Social Prophets for America of today."

Reagan brought these new issues and new battles and Rose Kryzak was ready to lead the battle against Reagan's policies. Within four months of taking office, Reagan found that his conservative mandate didn't extend to Social Security. Reagan proposed a massive tax cut and he proposed major cuts in government spending, including in Social Security. Many supporters of Social Security were wary of him. During the presidential campaign, an issue had been made of his previously-stated position that Social Security should be voluntary. To Rose, Reagan was not to be trusted. She and other seniors believed that any attempt to make Social Security voluntary would turn it into a welfare program and destroy public confidence in it.

Actually, Reagan's actions on Social Security were not without precedent. As the country was slipping into deficit spending during the recession and as Social Security faced fiscal problems with high interest rates causing the automatic cost of living adjustments to skyrocket, President Carter had proposed a number of cuts in the program which were denounced by seniors across the country. StateWide had even sent a telegram to Carter urging him not to agree to cuts in the cost of living adjustment in budget negotiations with Congress.

And, President Carter faced a mutiny in his own party as Senator

Edward Kennedy decided his moment had come to run for the White House. Rose had become very disenchanted with Carter as had many on the left in the Democratic Party. Rose decided to support Kennedy as he challenged Carter for the Democratic nomination in 1980. Rose especially liked Kennedy's more ambitious goals and legislation he sponsored that would move the country closer to universal health care. He would come to New York to campaign in the primary and Rose was there with him. He became enchanted with her and remarked that there was no one better to introduce him than Rose Kryzak. With his strong support in New York City, he rolled past Carter to win the New York primary.

The threat to Social Security at that time was so real that a new coalition was born, Seniors for Adequate Security. It began holding meetings around the state and nation. Rose reported in StateWide's newsletter on one of those meetings in 1979:

"On *March 16, 1979, a cold day, over 3000 elderly met at 13 Astor Place, New York City, to protest President Carter's attempted attack on the Social Security system. Both the audience and the speakers made it perfectly clear that the Social Security benefits are not to be tampered with. They are our rights, we worked for them, we earned them. The whole New York Congressional delegation either spoke at the rally or sent messages of support. There were additional speakers from senior citizens organizations, trade unions, community and fraternal organizations. Some speakers called for a march to Washington which was enthusiastically received. There was an atmosphere of determination that the Social Security system must be saved and improved and that we have just begun to fight.*"

Social Security was everything that Rose Kryzak believed in her entire life, a means for all persons, especially those with no other income to have some economic security. Defending the program was a natural and classic issue for her. She had been championing the cause since the 1930's and reminisced about the early days of the struggle:

I remember the time that there was no Social Security, no health care and we had to take care of our families, our parents. Did you know that there was a filial law that parents can sue children? It was a terrible thing because it tore families apart, it tore communities apart. People were so upset if a family was being sued. Children were so divided. Filial law allowed parents to sue children for support.

I remember when Reagan took office and he tried to institute the same law and on Channel 4 (New York City NBC affiliate). I said it was an outrageous proposal. It never passed. Before Social Security, you went to the poor house. The poor house was a city-run place. It was considered the worst thing if you had to face the poor house. It had a reputation and a feeling of destitution and depression. So, we used to always say, 'Well, we just want to be sure we don't get to the poor house'.

We had a campaign where people needed help. We used to go around and open the utility boxes. You know, people didn't pay their utility bill and so they would be shut out. We found a way to open the utility and we did. We did a lot of things to help each other. But if we ever got caught we'd be in big trouble, but we never got caught. You didn't need very much. For instance, when you called a doctor for my father or my mother, it was $2.00 but when you only earned $10 that's a lot of money. As little as it was, it was still a burden.

It got to a point when FDR talked about changes, people flocked to him. I went to many rallies. He used to draw tremendous crowds. He had very many creative ideas on how to help the people.

We had many demonstrations for Social Security. I remember the biggest rally very late in the campaign. They had about 30,000 people going from 23rd Street to Cit Hall. And, I was working at 150 Nassau Street. I went on the march, I took the time off. When I got to City Hall, I worked on the corner. I left the parade and went upstairs and I could see down on the demonstration. The leaders were going to have a rally. The anti-Social Security element came down on them. They attacked them. They beat them. They wouldn't let them have the rally. People were laid out on City Hall steps because they were injured. The anti- (Social Security) forces had the support of the police.

The people for it were tremendous. It was very close to when he signed the bill. I remember when FDR used to get pink letters, letters with pink paper, to show him he was a "red."

All I remember is when my father got his first Social Security check. - $50 was the minimum that my father got. There was a tremendous celebration in the community. That was the first check that came and people went kissing and hugging each other because they'd won such a tremendous victory. And, it was a tremendous victory. I think this is the best program that exists in the country".

So, it was from this very personal experience that Rose was ready to fight any effort by the Reagan Administration to weaken Social Security and she distrusted the new President's intentions, remembering that he had once said he wanted to make the program voluntary.

The 1981 White House Conference on the Aging

The controversy over Reagan's budget cuts and Social Security policies were the back drop for the 1981 White House Conference on the Aging, held every ten years since the first conference in 1961. The first conference was chaired by Dr. Arthur Flemming who had served as Secretary of Health, Education and Welfare under President Eisenhower. Flemming went on to serve in the same capacity at the 1971 White House Conference as President Nixon's appointee. Nixon later appointed Dr. Flemming to head the Administration on Aging in the Department of Health, Education and Welfare. In 1981, Flemming served as a co-chair.

After Reagan's embarrassment on Social Security, the White House became very nervous that the December conference would turn into a Reagan-bashing conclave. Blatantly, they engaged in such serious damage control that the conference became a political battleground. Delegates appointed by the states couldn't be unappointed, but Reagan's people could add more to pack the conference with Republican seniors. They could change the rules to control the agenda and stifle public dissent. So, they tried. The conference turned into a bitter battle by those who opposed Reagan's policies against a carefully orchestrated podium run rigidly by White House supporters.

The New York State Office for the Aging had been preparing for the participation of New York seniors for over a year and in May, a Governor's Conference on the Aging was held in Albany with over 600 persons attending. In Washington, the New York delegation led by Lou Glasse, Director of the State Office for the Aging, attempted any way it could to have a real debate and discussion about the issues.

Prior to the conference, the Reagan Administration went to

work to try and take full control over what happened at the conference. On Columbus Day weekend seniors and other delegates already picked to attend got telephone calls from persons saying they worked for the conference. They asked the delegates a number of personal questions and then asked their positions on issues. The persons who were calling were from a phone bank hired by the conference officials. Leora Hills, wife of StateWide President Reverend Howard Hills reported the call she received to Jane Gould who was the coordinator of the New York delegation.

Jane started making calls to New York delegates and found that a substantial number had been contacted by the phone bank operation. Information began to be gathered and when *The New York Times* reporter Warren Weaver began to look into it, he discovered that the Republican National Committee was behind the effort. The Democrats controlled the House of Representatives and Congressman Claude Pepper held hearings. Republican members of Congress insisted that affidavits be signed by individuals who received the calls.

The intent of the effort was to add delegates to change the makeup of those attending. They wanted people more committed to Reagan than to a senior agenda. The Reagan Administration also orchestrated the rules, requiring that delegates would have only one vote on the entire set of recommendations, rather than any separate voting on specific sections. Richard Schweiker, Secretary of Health and Human Services, said it was "simply not feasible" to allow votes on every report from fourteen different issue committees. He said that democracy would prevail though with lively discussions in those committees.

On the day the conference began, *The New York Times* editorialized:

"The Administration should know better than to treat the elderly like children. Recognizing the delegates' legitimate concern about Social Security, Medicare and other programs, the White House could use the conference as a chance to make its best case to an important audience. Ideally, both sides would learn something.

Instead, the wrangling over a politicized conference risks offending many of the nation's 26 million older adults. Contrary to stereotypes, a recent study shows, they are well-educated, healthy and politically able."

President Reagan himself decided to speak at the conference and used his charm on the crowd, uttering a memorable line, "maybe you can understand my frustration over the last couple of years – during my campaign and now in this office I hold – to be portrayed as somehow an enemy of my own generation." Reagan went on to note that the attack derived from one issue, Social Security, and said his opponents "cruelly" frightened older people with their demagoguery about his policies on the issue. Others noted that while the President got a pleasant reception, Congressman Claude Pepper of Florida, viewed as the foremost advocate for seniors, got a hero's welcome. Delegates chanted, "No more fraud, we want Claude."

The New York suite at the conference turned into the media center. The media reported Jane saying there were no microphones, no way to speak. She said there was going to be trouble, and she and the New York delegation began reaching out to other state delegations to protest the tight control of the conference and to insist on floor microphones. They wrote notes on pink paper and were accused of being Communists because of the color. As soon as the conference began, the New York delegation would seek to be recognized to force a vote to change the rules for voting on the recommendations. However, they didn't know if they would be recognized or ruled out of order. Jane asked Matt Schoenwald, President of the New York State Council of Senior Citizens, if he would stand out in the aisle. So, he stood up on chairs demanding to be heard, throwing fists in the air.

Jane called State Democratic Chair John Burns and asked him to get bullhorns and they got a company in Virginia to supply them. Assemblyman Paul Harenberg, Vito Lopez, a senior center leader from Brooklyn and Corey Sandler of the State Office for the Aging had bullhorns. They made huge signs. Jane had a microphone with a battery-operated box that she hid under her coat. She asked Rose to speak and warned other delegations what might happen. Lou Glasse didn't want to do this but Jane and the delegates wanted to take action. Rose and Jane stepped out into the aisle and Rose said, "This is not fair. We need a voice, we want to vote on independent resolutions."

Three security officers showed up and tried to wrestle the microphone from Rose but she held on while others nearby yelled not to touch her. Rose was hanging onto that microphone while others were hanging onto her, Rose shouted out for "ABC, CBS, NBC." Republicans from the Florida delegation helped to get men away from her. She and others were later interviewed about their anger at the way the conference was being run. They had exposed the rigged nature of it and the whole conference became a major media controversy and a political headache for the Reagan Administration.

The Conference security officers were so incensed that they started grabbing women's handbags and dumping them on the floor. One New York delegate said it was just like Nazi Germany. Jane Gould noted that Senator Moynihan, the most respected voice in the country on Social Security and human services, was furious with Lou Glasse, but Governor Carey was somewhat amused and did not reprimand the agency's leaders.

Reporting on the conference later in a newsletter, Lou Glasse wrote, "How did we succeed in including many good recommendations among the 600 finally adopted in a single vote? It was a combination of the media attention to the attempts at political meddling and the hard, resourceful efforts of older New Yorkers and others."

America magazine, a Catholic publication, editorialized after the conference,

"The delegates to the 1981 White House Conference on Aging reminded the nation's most powerful senior citizens that Americans who are 65 and over, and who constitute twenty-two percent of the population and an even larger proportion of the voters, reject as inconceivable the notion of returning to the Coolidge era of their childhood or youth. Over the past half-century, the federal government has assumed a key role in safeguarding the welfare of all citizens, and no one wants it to abdicate that responsibility. On the other hand, since the President and Congress must try to control inflationary federal spending, they would be justified in reminding older Americans that programs for the aged already account for about twenty-five percent of the astronomical federal budget. There is an obvious and painful dilemma here that must be acknowledged if it is ever to be resolved."

Scarred by the battle, Reagan and lawmakers agreed that the only politically safe way to handle Social Security reform was to appoint a bipartisan commission that would be somewhat insulated from Congressional politics while it deliberated. This commission had many prominent political leaders on it including Senator Bob Dole and Senator Moynihan and it was chaired by Alan

Greenspan. Eventually the commission approved a plan to strengthen Social Security by gradually delaying the retirement age for full benefits to 67 by the year 2027, eliminating temporarily the cost-of-living adjustment, increasing the payroll tax and raising the wage ceiling subject to it.

The plan was approved in Congress and it extended the life of the Trust Fund for many years as projected at that time. It was a compromise that StateWide's board of directors voted to endorse "with reservations" in 1983, particularly raising the retirement age to 67 in the future and delaying the cost of living adjustment (COLA) for six months. They endorsed it not because they liked it, but because "members of the board felt that...it was necessary to endorse the proposal so that conservative opponents would not be able to defeat it and then seek even more drastic negative changes" as the position was described at the time.

Rose had a visceral dislike for Reagan and she continued to speak out and work against his policies. At StateWide's 1983 convention in Syracuse, she spoke on a panel discussion about Medicare and delivered the kind of vintage remarks that she was known for:

"Three years of the Reagan Administration have been a disaster for the elderly, disabled and the poor. The elderly lost benefits that took years to achieve. We are approaching the fourth year of the Reagan administration and we must pledge to make it his last year...Is health care a benefit for the rich only? Or is it a right, along with public education and police and fire protection?... Reagan has declared war on the elderly, the disabled and the poor. The present administration will be remembered for cutting human services and raising the military budget. A $248.9 billion military budget is no guarantee of maximum national security. The best

guarantee of national security is a population that is well fed, well clothed, well housed and in good health. This is an election year and the elderly are in no one's pockets...Finally, I have a question for you to answer... Do you believe that we, the elderly, who partic004ipated in building the richest country in the world with its vast resources, should be able to live out the remaining years of our lives in decency, dignity and in good health?"

When Reagan ran for re-election in 1984, the Democratic state committee produced a pamphlet, *The Plot to Kill Social Security*. And, Rose continued to speak out about Reagan's policies. In that election year, her Congresswoman Geraldine Ferraro of Queens became the head of the Democratic Party's Platform Committee and Rose was invited to make a presentation on April 9th to the Committee. The Congresswoman sent her a note of thanks. In a few months, Ferraro was nominated by Walter Mondale as the first woman to ever be on the ticket of one of the two major parties. Rose liked Ferraro personally but would come to feel she was too conservative for her.

Social Security's 50th Birthday

Social Security continued to be a political issue after Reagan won re-election by a landslide in 1984. In 1985, seniors were not just celebrating the 50th anniversary of Social Security but also still trying to defend the program against budget cuts. A Congressional proposal to eliminate the Social Security cost of living adjustment (COLA) for January 1, 1986 became a political hot potato. StateWide joined a national "Birthday Card" campaign with other New York advocacy groups which together sent thousands of cards to the state's Congressional delegation, saying, "Don't Cut the COLA." On April 10, 1985, members of StateWide brought the press along and delivered a Social Security birthday cake to the Albany office of Senator Alfonse D'Amato. Similar "birthday parties" were held all over the country.

On August 14, 1985, thousands of seniors from across the state were bused by labor unions and other organizations to FDR's estate at Hyde Park for the 50th anniversary of the signing of the Social Security Act. It was a warm summer day as they fanned out across the vast estate. The celebration was sponsored by the coalition, Save our Security (SOS), which had been formed in 1978 to defend the program. Many were union members and warriors in many social justice crusades. They were fiercely loyal to Social Security and ready to fight those who might try to alter its social insurance foundation. Most of the seniors could remember the passage of the bill a half century earlier and they came to celebrate what they viewed as the most important government program ever established.

Like Rose Kryzak, Max Manes, another long-time senior activist, recalled how difficult it was to be a hatmaker in the 1930's. In celebrating the 50th anniversary, he wrote about the struggle for income security back then:

"I remember when Social Security was enacted, and I remember the joy with which it was welcomed. Like workers in other industries, we in the men's hats, members of the old United Hatters of North America, now part of the Amalgamated Clothing and Textile Workers, felt strongly the need for a national system of social insurance and we made ourselves heard on it. Working in seasonal industry with chronic slack periods and layoffs, with no unemployment insurance and no pensions for the aged, we knew what it meant to lose the normal source of income. Those among us who could no longer work and sought assistance from official

agencies were subjected to a degrading means test to prove need, and their children had to prove they were unable to support them before their parents could qualify for any assistance. A benefit for widows or other survivors, which was paid for them from union dues collapsed after the Wall Street crash as did similar such plans in other industries. For us, the enactment of Social Security was like a dream come true. This mainstay for retirees, the disabled and survivors of covered workers must be preserved."

There, on the steps of Springwood, Roosevelt's family home, just a few feet from the graves of Eleanor and Franklin Roosevelt, the living leaders of the movement for Social Security gathered to celebrate the program. The honorary co-chairmen of the celebration were Franklin D. Roosevelt, Jr. and Robert Wagner, the former New York City Mayor and son of the Senator who had sponsored the Social Security Act. Governor Cuomo gave the keynote address with other remarks by Congressman Claude Pepper, former Health Education and Welfare Secretary Arthur Flemming.

For FDR, Social Security was an extension of the retirement fund he established as governor of New York, the first social insurance retirement pension in the country.

Cuomo was eloquent as always:

"For the 50 years since President Franklin Delano Roosevelt signed the Social Security Act, millions of Americans have known that Social Security works. We have sustained it with contributions from the fruits of our labor, defended it against those who would take it away from people in need and improved it for the security of future generations. FDR knew 50 years ago what we all know now - that Social Security is in the mainstream of the American philosophy of social responsibility in action. FDR once

said that the social objectives of his administration were to do 'what any honest government of any country would do: to try to increase the security and happiness of a larger number of people in all occupations of life and in all parts of the country — to give them assurance that they are not going to starve in old age.' We still subscribe to those goals today."

Chapter Six

"Red" and Gray

It was also in the early 1980's, that Rose Kryzak became a main character in another media event. A documentary, Seeing Red, was produced about the old Communist movement in the United States. Along with folk singer Pete Seeger, Rose Kryzak was one of the twelve persons extensively profiled. The movie would be shown on public television and when Rose appeared speaking at a senior citizens rally in New York, a subtitle appeared below on the screen that said that Rose was one of only two of the twelve who were still active members of the party. It came as a surprise to many people who knew her only from her senior advocacy work. She explained it in the film:

"It was a decision I had to make, a lot of work I do is either federally or state funded. They could say they can't have a known Communist, but then, I said, if I die, why shouldn't there be a record? How could I have been so good when I was so active and be so bad because I tell that I was a Communist. I felt I owe to everybody who knows me to know who I was and who I am and why I am doing what I am."

Rose was concerned about the movie, recalled friend Bill Arnone who had worked with her when he was with the New York City Department for Aging and remained a good friend. She was more concerned about whether the revelation of her past would hurt some of her friends in the senior advocacy movement.

Bill recalled a humorous story Rose told him of how at her desk at Buck Associates she would read the Communist Party paper, *The Daily Worker*, holding it inside the *International Herald Tribune*. One day, her boss called her into the office and told her that she would have to stop reading the paper at her desk. She was worried now as she thought she had been found out. She said she wouldn't read it anymore. Then, her boss continued, "You know the International Herald Tribune is a very left-wing paper!" Rose got a great laugh telling that story and wondering what Mr. Buck would think if he really knew what she was reading. Later in the 1950's though he would stand up for her when questioned about her by the FBI.

Though Rose would call herself a Communist with all its inflammatory connotations, the reality was that by substituting the phrase, "democratic Socialist" you had a better description of what Rose Kryzak was in her years as a senior activist.

In fact, among the liberal senior activists in the 1970's and 1980's there were several who had been active in the Communist Party in their youth. There were others in StateWide, especially labor leaders like Helen Quirini at General Electric in Schenectady who were suspected of being Communists. Helen had been questioned by Roy Cohn and Senator Joseph McCarthy about her knowledge of Communists in the union. She was just as feisty and combative with Cohn and McCarthy as she would be later as a senior advocate.

Mr. Cohn: Do you think that Mr. Matles and Mr. Emspak, two of the top officials of the UE (union) do you think they are not Communists?

Miss Quirini: I have no idea whether they are or not.

The Chairman: You do not mean that?

Miss Quirini: I do mean that.

The Chairman: Do you mean you do not know if Emspak is a Communist?

Miss Quirini: I don't know. How am I supposed to know?

The Chairman: Have you ever heard they were Communists?

Miss Quirini: I have heard a lot of people were Communists.

The Chairman: Have you ever heard that they were Communists?

Miss Quirini: I have heard they were Communists.

The Chairman: You have heard it repeatedly, have you not?

Miss Quirini: That is right. I have heard it about myself, too, though Senator.

To understand Rose Kryzak's feelings about Communism, you have to remember the world she was born into. When Lenin had taken over in the Bolshevik Revolution, it was a positive change to Rose and her family after the years of poverty and oppression of the Jews under the czars. Like many people, she was filled with admiration for the Communist revolution and experiment and in the 1930's she actively supported socialist causes in the United States. Rose's son Tom remarked, "They (his parents) considered themselves pioneers, going down the road that this country should go down.... She held to her belief throughout her life...partly it was patriotism for the old country."

Rose returned to her homeland in 1933. It was the Soviet Union then and the czar was long gone. She found a cousin of hers and was amazed at how much better things were than what she remembered as a child. Her cousin's children went to the university and traveled freely. When Rose was growing up, no one in the family could read or go to school. Jews also had more freedom under the

Communists. Anti-Semitism was never completely wiped out but was punished by law. She returned to Russia four times to visit her cousins. She was always impressed that there was no fear on the streets, no unemployment, and buildings were going up. Everything seemed okay.

When she got back, Franklin D. Roosevelt was the new President and Rose campaigned for Social Security and joined the Communist Party in 1933. Party representatives were surprised because people just didn't come in off the street to sign up. She loved the idealism of the Communist Party. She became a local organizer in Sunnyside, Queens and it became a central part of her life:

"I tell you I could cry thinking of the excitement; the pride we had. We just marched through the streets with the pride that we are the people that count. May Day was such a holiday. I remember when our children were little, we used to carry them on our shoulder. There was something that we were so excited about, it meant so much to us."

When Khrushchev denounced Stalin and revealed the extent of his brutality in the 1950's, many left the US party. Rose did not. She said that she felt it was wrong to renounce her membership as if she had to admit a wrong on her part. She still felt its goals were right even if its very human leaders failed to follow the spirit of the revolution for the people's benefit:

"You can't throw everything out, Stalin did a lot for the revolution and after all he did participate in building the revolution. Now what happened in the subsequent years where he made a very serious mistake and did harm in many ways - if you are going

to use that as a basis to be in or out - then you're really losing sight of the main objective of the Communist revolution."

She was quite doctrinaire in supporting communism, though it is hard to envision her ever supporting violence to deny human rights. Her involvement led her to dangerous roads in later years when Senator Joseph McCarthy seized control of the nation's agenda and Rose and her friends became his targets. Rose's brother was near the top of the FBI's list and he went into hiding. Rose told him she didn't want to know where he was so that if she was asked by the FBI she could say without lying that she didn't know.

All around her, there was evidence of the pressure. The FBI followed her.

"I had to sit down and talk to my children that they might be accosted, that they know that their mother and father never did anything wrong, that whatever we did was to help the community."

My brother was underground. So, they always bothered me because they thought I'd be the one to know. I was happy I didn't know because I remember saying, God, they could torture my children and I'd have to tell the truth, but if I don't know, they could pull my tongue out and I couldn't tell them. I was very secure that I never knew where he was. He came out of hiding and we were very happy. We took care of his children and his wife. I used to ask (my son) Tommy, What would you like for your birthday?" He'd say, 'I want Bill to come home.. To get rid of his cousins!'

And, when Ethel and Julius Rosenberg were executed in 1953 for spying for the Soviet Union, she helped find a family to adopt their children.

"The children stayed somewhere near Pennsylvania and we wanted them to be taken by a couple who wanted to take care of them. To do it, we had to make sure that the people who were going to do it were going to be reliable. So, they interviewed the people who agreed to take them and they interviewed me and I agreed to give them a teacher in the nursery school who would supervise the care of the children and everybody agreed to everything and the two children were taken by this couple and they grew up with them and later on they tried to vindicate the Rosenbergs. No, I didn't know them (Rosenbergs). I was involved to get the nursery school teacher in a secondary way. They know if they need somebody like that, they would call me and that I would get it for them. They knew that I was caring, very caring and I would do it and I did."

During the McCarthy era, Rose had other harrowing experiences. She and other members of the party went to Peekskill, New York in 1949 for a summer concert featuring Paul Robeson, the world renowned African-American singer and actor and leader in the Civil Rights movement. Robeson would sing every year at these concerts, which benefited the Civil Rights Congress. Robeson though had just created an international uproar with a speech in Paris in which he said, "It is unthinkable that the Negro people of America or elsewhere...would be drawn into war with the Soviet Union.

When word spread about Robeson's upcoming concert in Peekskill, anti-Communist sentiment was whipped up by the local paper, business groups, veteran's groups and the assistant district attorney, according to the book, Red Scare. Bumper stickers were distributed which said things like: "Communism is treason. Behind Communism Stands the Jew! Therefore: For My Country - Against the Jews!"

So a mob of rioters was ready for those who set out for a nice concert in the afternoon. Among those attending was Rose Kryzak:

"Paul Robeson had a concert...I think I had my daughter with me, and my sister-in-law. It was a picnic. And we had a wonderful day and it was jammed. And everybody at the picnic was warned, when you go home, and (when) you get out of the park, keep your windows closed.

After we came through the Newport bridge (they) threw rocks at the car and broke windows and injured people and the police did nothing to stop them. A lot of people were injured. I just took my daughter and just pushed her down. Well I didn't get hurt, but my sister-in law got hurt on the arm. Yeah, we had to take her to the hospital down the road. It reminded me of the time of the pogrom. They were ruthless.

Yes, Paul Robeson sang at the picnic, he was one of the singers and there were speeches haranguing him and I was thinking, gee, What is this? You know, and then he sings Old Man River but all the words were changed so that it was a political statement which of course, it is the kind of song you can make a political statement out of because it is about oppression."

Griffin Fariello notes in *Red Scare* that the attacks left 215 injured, 145 of those were hospitalized and twenty-five were arrested. He noted that Governor Thomas Dewey later characterized the concert goers as "the shock troops of a revolutionary force" and ordered a grand jury investigation to determine whether the concert was "part of the Communist strategy to foment racial and religious hatred."

Rose was one of those people who had the courage to endure the McCarthy era with her conscience and integrity intact. She was a woman who wanted deeply for every person to have the economic necessities of life. That was what she had been fighting for in those years and when I met her decades later. She remained only nominally active in the Communist Party even though it still existed. She wasn't distancing herself from the party and she viewed the party as part of her life, especially in the past and she never felt the need to renounce her past. She still defended the original socialist ideals of the Communist Party rather than the brutal repressive dictatorships in the Soviet Union and other countries in the Cold War. It seemed though that, being such a practical person, she knew that the Communist Party really had no influence or power on the legislative issues she wanted to work on, so she was active in mainstream political vehicles whether they be senior organizations or supporting Democrats. In fact, the party often took credit for her work with others in *The Daily Worker.*

CHAPTER SEVEN

MARIO CUOMO
AND THE FAMILY OF NEW YORK

S TATEWIDE'S CONVENTIONS WERE ALWAYS AN ATTRACTION FOR STATE
political figures with higher aspirations who wanted to establish relationships with organized interest groups. An invitation to
speak at StateWide's annual convention was appealing for many
because they enjoyed speaking to seniors and wanted to offer a
positive agenda to a reliable constituency that voted. In 1980, a little
known Congresswoman from Queens named Geraldine Ferraro
attended StateWide's convention in Syracuse. She had recently won
election to Congress but she was not well known like New York
City's trio of nationally known women in Congress: Bella Abzug,
Shirley Chisholm and Elizabeth Holtzman. One person who got
around a lot to speak to various organizations was the new lieutenant governor, 47-year-old Mario Cuomo who took office in
1979. He was also from Rose Kryzak's borough of Queens. He
went to Syracuse to speak to StateWide's conventions in 1980 and
1981.

Most of the political analysts in Albany, the legislators and
even the governors don't take lieutenant governors too seriously.
They are subject to the same jokes as vice presidents are in
Washington. Being lieutenant governor was a job that had little

power except to preside over the State Senate and being available to serve the governor's interests at various events. He had the title of lieutenant governor so he, at least, was coveted as a speaker and he worked hard to court various groups. Like any Democratic state office holder looking for higher office, Cuomo was well known and accessible to the statewide community associations, particularly those working on human services issues. He sent his staff out to keep contact with them. He seemed to always show up at the conferences of the human services groups and other community organizations. There was Mario speaking with 50 people at a rural housing conference. There was Mario with his church friends at the Labor/Religion conference at a Catholic retreat house. There was Mario speaking at the StateWide convention. He and his staff mingled with the people and they loved him.

Mario Cuomo had a golden throat and was one of those few speakers who could excite and move people's emotions. No one who had ever heard Cuomo speak could ever forget him. And, he certainly could do that for older people with his stories of his immigrant parents and their struggles coming to America. He always spoke about "Momma and Poppa," and how the country had been good to them. At a time when liberalism was left lurching in self-doubt, Mario Cuomo was a man who felt all those things deeply.

He talked about the morality of helping the poor. His success was tied to his ability to articulate and touch the chords of the past that said there was something of value about our ancestors, that we were part of a bigger picture, that those uneducated immigrants who came and worked so hard were the people we should be making policy for. He could put it in words, he could make you jump to your feet. He could make some people cry.

In 1981, in the first year of the Reagan Administration, when most Democrats and liberals were on the defensive, Cuomo's speech to the StateWide convention stood out because it challenged the prevailing conservative era. He denounced the "macho politics" and the "new conservatism" of Reagan and venerated the generation of the immigrants like his parents who had "built this nation." "Such people would have us leave the elderly to fend for themselves. They say, 'Knock out the crutches, they'll learn to walk'." He had the crowd in the palm of his hands as he rebutted the whole notion of Reaganomics and budget cutting,

"Fiscal soundness is essential and balanced budgets to achieve it are legally mandated. But the purpose of government is to make reasonably secure the conditions of people's lives. If it fails to do that, it fails utterly, no matter how neatly symmetrical the columns of its ledgers. A Triple A bond rating for a state that has failed to meet its basic needs would be the emblem of hypocrisy. All efforts at austerity should be viewed, ultimately, in that light."

In that speech he praised the past accomplishments of the Democratic administration he was a part of and laid out an agenda for further action which notably included prescription drug relief legislation, abolition of mandatory retirement, increasing the level of the state share to supplement SSI and promotion of cheaper generic drugs.

It was not only a defense of traditional Democratic policies to help the poor and the less fortunate. Cuomo went further and blasted the philosophical underpinnings of Reaganomics, calling it "social Darwinism" in which government's role of protecting and helping the less fortunate was reduced and that survival of the fittest in the marketplace ruled.

Mario Cuomo was always willing to defend and champion the cause of the poor, stirring souls and leaving people in awe with his convictions. A year earlier, just after Reagan was elected in November 1980, Cuomo told the New York Association of Human Services at its annual convention in Syracuse, "Since Adam and Eve conspired to eat the apple, man has not been able to be trusted in helping his fellow man. If he were, we wouldn't have needed child labor laws or unions. Human nature needs a little nudging to help others. It is the function of government to do that." Cuomo called for a commitment to family and community. It was the same basis of the speech he gave just four years later as the keynoter at the 1984 Democratic National Convention that catapulted him into national prominence. Those who heard him in those lieutenant governor years were not surprised by his San Francisco triumph.

No one talked about Cuomo's future in those days. By 1980, he and Hugh Carey were moving further apart. Cuomo was state chairman for Jimmy Carter's re-election campaign. Carey wasn't enthralled with Carter. He flirted with running for president and then withheld his support of Carter for a while. By 1981, Carey was becoming more and more a figure of ridicule, almost a joke, as he dated and then married the wealthy Evangeline Gouletas. The media had a field day reporting that she had been married once before, then twice before. Carey didn't know her complete past. Meanwhile, she was making Carey feel more youthful, dying his hair. Invited to the Governor's mansion on Senior Citizens' Day, Rose Kryzak was stunned when Carey came in with the same orange hair that was the subject of great fun in the media.

Cuomo seemed to sense the discontent with Carey and began saying publicly that he was definitely going to run for something in 1982. He didn't necessarily mean governor, but it looked that way. It was the first sign of one of Cuomo's habits of teasing the public and stirring speculation about running for higher office. He recounted it all in his diaries and apparently was ready to run for governor. So there was the specter of Carey and Cuomo facing each other.

Then in early 1982, Carey said he wouldn't run again and it seemed that Cuomo might become the frontrunner. Other state officials thought about running. Assembly Speaker Stanley Fink was prominently mentioned. He was the favorite of those working in the Legislature and that gave him a powerful base in the party across the state with nearly 100 fellow Democratic Assemblymembers. Attorney General Robert Abrams was mentioned along with State Senate Minority Leader Manhred Ohrenstein. Ed Koch wasn't mentioned because he had just been re-elected Mayor of New York City by a landslide in 1981. He loved that job and didn't seem interested in being governor. However, within days, Koch decided he'd like to be governor and he announced his candidacy and instantly was favored to win the nomination.

Other potential candidates except Cuomo bowed out as the media and the party professionals conceded the election to Koch. So, a re-match was set between the two who had faced each other in the primary for New York City Mayor in 1977. Many public officials in the Carey Administration cast their lot with Koch because they thought Koch would win and they wanted to keep their jobs in state government or get better ones, and Cuomo didn't forget whom they were. It was like they were betting on horses. Forget ideology, political conviction or personality. Go for the winner. The media and the Democratic establishment had a coronation for Koch.

Some weren't so sure it was going to be a runaway though. Liberals in the party supported Cuomo and they turned out in primary elections. Then, there were the upstaters who Cuomo knew through his work with local governments as Secretary of

State. Cuomo worked hard and won the support of many liberal constituencies including minority groups and unions, which were offended with some of Koch's policies in the city.

Before long, Koch began to self-destruct when he insulted Albany's lack of variety in international cuisine, derided rural life in upstate farm areas and forgot what county he was speaking in when visiting Oneonta. So, on primary night in September, Cuomo pulled off a big upset though to many who were so impressed with him, his victory was not all that surprising.

Cuomo, still not all that well known upstate, had to immediately begin the general election campaign against the wealthy conservative Lew Lehrman who had never held office but had become a household word with his multi-million dollar ad campaign during the Republican primary. He had become easily recognized with his red suspenders and can-do business-like attitude. He wanted to bring Reaganomics to New York and Cuomo was glad to run against Reagan with the country in a recession and Reagan's popularity down.

While non-profit senior organizations like StateWide could not endorse candidates for office, Cuomo had the support of many senior leaders and advocates though Rose Kryzak did not sign on to a flyer, "Older New Yorkers Need MARIO CUOMO" listing his supporters. That flyer said, "As Governor of New York, I will defend Social Security and Medicare from those who would destroy it." It listed a number of programs and policies Cuomo supported including:

- the elimination of mandatory retirement policies in the public and private sector
- an annual increase in SSI benefits and in the personal care allowance for residents of nursing homes and adult homes

- establishing a statewide prescription drug insurance program for older persons
- fighting to keep senior centers open
- support of bills in the State Legislature to prevent automatic rent increases for tenants
- a criminal justice system, which works, which catches, convicts and jails the criminal who preys on older people. Life sentences without parole for those convicted of heinous crimes.

The polls showed Cuomo with a slim lead during the next few weeks and he maintained it. When Cuomo debated Lehrman, his lawlerly instincts and logical arguments shredded Lehrman. With the country still in a recession, Republicans took a beating across the country and Cuomo squeaked by Lehrman 51%-48%.

StateWide Moves to Albany

Just before Cuomo was moving into the governor's office, StateWide made a big transition and moved its main office to Albany. StateWide had a glorious run of almost a decade until Ronald Reagan came into office and did away with the Community Services Administration, which had provided most of the organization's funding. Anti-poverty money was cut, particularly for advocacy by citizens groups. After over eight years on the job launching StateWide, Bob O'Donnell, resigned to accept a position with a national organization serving the blind. StateWide was without a director for many months though the Rochester communications office continued to function and run the organization. Two seniors on Bob's staff, Viola Thompson and Elizabeth Van Horn, worked in spaced donated by Marine Midland Bank. Vi had been Bob's personal assistant even though they were many miles away. Another office in Syracuse was closed along with the Albany office that worked on energy issues. StateWide's survival in 1981 was largely due to Assembly Speaker Stanley Fink who was a supporter of senior organizations and gave StateWide a $60,000 "member item" special grant in the state budget.

With StateWide clinging for life, the board of directors formed a search committee and decided to move the main office to Albany. Knowing me from my work with seniors in the Albany area on energy issues, the board agreed to hire me upon the recommendation of Reverend Hills and the local seniors. I said yes in an instant. I had actually worked for StateWide briefly as a consultant on energy issues when I had moved to Albany from Watertown in 1979. So, I was very familiar with the organization when I began working in September 1982 to prepare for the annual convention, which was held in early November. I was only 29, but to the board members, my youth and ability to devote my energies to the job were assets. I had spent a year and a half at the State Office for the Aging as a housing and energy policy analyst, but it was not a good role for me. StateWide was a grassroots organization and much more suited for me than working for the state government.

Indeed, it didn't seem an accident that I would work for an organization like StateWide. Growing up in an Italian-American family, my brother and my other cousins and I revered our grandparents and their generation who had left the poverty of Calabria in southern Italy to find a better life in upstate New York. My mother's father came to Massena in northern New York on the Canadian border to work in the Alcoa aluminum plant before he later started his own Italian restaurant. My father's family came from Calabria and settled in Rochester. When I left college at St. Lawrence University I wanted to get a job working to help the poor and the elderly in the community. Doing something that would help those in need if they needed it by expanding assistance for health care, long-term care, heating aid and housing had a great appeal to me.

So, the job to run this organization became mine and with it trying to learn quickly how to raise more money. Fortunately, it was also at that time that a wealthy progressive named Phillippe Villers of Boston decided to donate $40 million to start a new foundation that would be focused on the needs of older persons, funding local groups involved in advocacy and organizing for social change. StateWide was a perfect match and became one of the first grantees of the new Villers Foundation. The foundation money that continued for several years gave StateWide some financial stability in addition to the funds, which continued to come from state government. Eventually grant money was no longer given by the Villers Foundation and the remaining money was used to create a new national advocacy organization, Families USA which continues today as a foremost advocate on health care issues. The New York Foundation became a major supporter of StateWide for many years.

In my new position I got quickly re-acquainted with Rose Kryzak, I had actually met Rose a few years earlier at other StateWide functions. And, I had heard of her long before I met her. I first had read about the "Kryzak problem" in an energy newsletter in 1976 when she spoke at the Federal Power Commission. She remembered first meeting me at a conference on rural elderly in Lake Placid in 1980. She remembered, though I didn't, that I had held up a sign saying, "Clone Rose Kryzak." She found that quite amusing and flattering. After I got to know her, I found her to be a natural leader with an irresistible charm and power to take over a meeting with the force of her personality.

Rose became my Jewish grandmother and I viewed myself as her "agent." In the years that followed we literally became like family. When I first became Executive Director of StateWide I was single, but after I was married and had children, Rose often stayed at our house on trips to Albany and twice when we went to New York for weddings, we spent the weekends and left our son with Rose and her granddaughter for the day. And, every Thanksgiving when Rose went to visit her children in New Jersey, they took her to a department store and she bought and sent holiday gifts for our kids - clothes always much bigger than they were, because she wanted to be sure they would last a while.

CHAPTER EIGHT

ALBANY IN THE CUOMO YEARS

MARIO CUOMO WAS INAUGURATED ON JANUARY 1, 1983 AND delivered an emotional and stunning address about the Family of New York that he had been giving to groups across the state. The next day, thousands of people stood in the cold for a chance to enter the Governor's Mansion and shake the hand of the new governor. Cuomo appointed his friend, Dr. Eugene Callender, an African-American minister who was a friend to be the new Director of the State Office for the Aging. Jane Gould was promoted to Executive Deputy Director.

It didn't take long after Cuomo took office to learn that the government was not just one man, that "the state," the bureaucracy, was more entrenched than he was. His soaring rhetoric about the poor had built high expectations among those who worked in human needs. There was a feeling that Cuomo was a white knight who understood poverty and the underside of life and who would shake things up by overruling the bureaucrats when they didn't do the right thing or at least when they went against the wishes of grassroots groups. Cuomo had to be dependent though on those who had experience in state government and he ended up re-appointing many of those who had served with Hugh Carey, the professional managers.

So, it was inevitable perhaps that advocacy organizations representing grassroots organizations might come into conflict with state agency managers. StateWide had an on-going battle with the State Social Services Department (DSS) about the operation of the Home Energy Assistance Program (HEAP) since it began. DSS had used Reagan's new federalism of block grants and exercised the option to transfer up to ten percent of funding from one block grant to other uses. So, as funds were cut back in other areas they used the heating funds to pay for other social services programs.

The money was needed for energy assistance and the state was just using the federal funds to replace state funds. After all, if the programs the state wanted to transfer money to were so important, it was argued, why didn't they come up with money from the state budget for them.

More people signed up and HEAP continued to expand. State officials had mismanaged the program so badly by transferring the money that in January of 1984, in the midst of the winter, funding for energy assistance was exhausted. I was outraged and we went to the press. I had developed a relationship with R. W. Groneman, a reporter for the *Schenectady Gazette* and he was relentless in pursuing the issue.

Finally, he brought it up to Cuomo in a press conference. Cuomo, who had charmed the press through the first year, seemed unfamiliar with the issue and defensive. With the issue now out in the open, the entire press corps got into it. The next day, *The New York Times* was on the line calling me. They were doing a story and wanted to go out to take a picture of someone who used the program but couldn't get help now that applications were unavailable. We sent them to Norwich near Utica where Pauline Kinney, a member of StateWide's board posed in front of her woodstove.

The media coverage snowballed. It was in all the papers after appearing on the wire service. Cuomo relied on his staff to respond.

They "found" $5 million in an emergency account to keep the program going. Meanwhile, I was set to leave for Ireland with twenty seniors on a four-day, discounted promotional tour intended by the travel agents to produce future senior trips. My brother joked that I caused all that trouble and then left the country. Finding the funds to continue the e program was another example of how when an issue has merit and it receives a lot of advocacy and media attention, public leaders, even governors, have to change their policies.

The energy issue wouldn't go away either. In January of 1985, the administration invited a number of legislators and advocates to a press conference. Joseph Kennedy, the eldest son of Bobby Kennedy was coming to Albany to announce how his Citizens Energy Corporation would offer lower cost natural gas to poor New York families.

A few hundred people crowded into the Blue Room at the State Capitol. All the fanfare went into a program which was going to help 18,000 families, while the state was fighting a lawsuit that could help 90,000 families get aid. Once again, the reporters saw a story. After two years of Cuomo they were starting to do stories about "the rhetoric and the reality."

Cuomo was the first to admit that prose and poetry were not the same. The poetry of giving speeches wasn't the same as the prose of governing. It was his defense of why the rhetoric and the reality didn't always congeal. The high rhetoric seemed a longing for the ideal, to seek values.

For a Democrat, he was the dream candidate, unlike any white politician since the Kennedys in his ability to stir the soul and capture an audience. We expected that when someone talked about the poor they would behave like Lyndon Johnson started to and that, at least he would be as obstinate about his priorities as Ronald Reagan was, that he would try to use his power. The proof of this was that Cuomo did occasionally use his power. Throughout his administration, he and his staff created the crusade of the year. They fought for a transportation bond issue. They fought for a higher drinking age, for ethics in government. He did announce a Decade of the Child and Liberty Scholarships. He did produce public housing. It took awhile though to pressure him and make him an advocate for senior issues.

In the early 1980's, three or four other issues dominated the senior agenda at the state level. Seniors had been pushing for seven years to ban mandatory retirement. To seniors, it was a civil rights issue. Mandatory retirement was age discrimination. As always in politics, there was another side which didn't see it that way. Big companies didn't want government to tell them what to do. In 1981, CBS News respected anchorman Walter Cronkite had to retire at the age of 65 because that was company policy. In the early 1980's the battle continued and every year, the Legislature would take no action even though a large number of seniors have been vocal in favor of the bill.

In 1974 Paul Harenberg, a teacher from Long Island, was elected to the State Assembly as a reformer. In 1982, he was appointed by Speaker Stanley Fink to be the new Chair of the Aging Committee. Soft-spoken but committed to pushing for progressive legislation to improve the plight of older persons, Harenberg became the leader in the Assembly for bills seniors wanted. He sponsored the legislation to ban mandatory retirement.

So, the Assembly Democrats passed a bill which outlawed mandatory retirement in public and private employment while the Senate bill sponsored by the Chair of the Aging Committee, Hugh Farley of Schenectady only outlawed mandatory retirement in public employment. Former Governor Carey had agreed with Farley as did New York City Mayor Ed Koch. Mario Cuomo, though, accepted the Assembly's and the advocates' position and Koch also switched. So, the pressure on the Senate intensified.

By 1984, senior advocates decided to step up the pressure even more. Each year, the Legislature designated the first Tuesday in May as Senior Citizens Day. Ceremonies were held by the governor and then the Legislature would hold a ceremony in the Legislative Office Building and present two awards to seniors in the state, including the Senior Citizen of the Year and the Outstanding Contribution award. In 1984, StateWide and other advocacy organizations decided to turn the event into a protest rally. Hundreds of seniors came to Albany that day and the message was delivered.

It was an election year and legislators were feeling the heat. So, in front of a big crowd with many protest signs, legislative leaders announced at the ceremony that a compromise had finally been reached on a new law that would end discrimination in hiring, promoting or terminating an individual 18 years of age or older. The bill exempted workers in jobs where age was found a "bonafide occupational qualification based on conclusive proof that advancing age is directly related to job performance." It also exempted private sector executives who reach age 65 and have an annual pension over $27,000 and tenured employees at college at age 70, certain state and New York City fire, police, corrections and sanitation officers who are members of retirement plans that permit immediate retirement upon twenty-five years of service. With that battle resolved, senior advocates were ready to focus on other issues on the agenda.

For Rose, 1985 was a very sad year. Her husband George died in the fall. They were on their annual vacation renting a housekeeping cottage on Lake George when he had a heart attack. Rose went with him and sat for days at the Glens Falls hospital. Her beloved Kay never went home though. Rose was a pragmatist and she knew she had to keep her mind on positive things, so her work became her outlet even more so during her sorrow. She didn't dwell on death though she knew it could come at any time. She was an atheist, but she was really a humanist. She would say that she had tried to live a good life and felt she had helped others. She felt that if there were a reward after death, she would certainly receive it.

Within the next year, she would sell the home she and her husband had enjoyed for many years. She decided to move to Flushing House in Queens, a senior residence which provided meals. Even though she and her husband had not been wealthy, they were able to live comfortably and she had the resources from selling the house and other savings to pay for the supportive services at Flushing House. She wanted to devote her remaining years to her senior advocacy work. There, she lived among her peers and always had firsthand experience of their problems. She became very popular with the residents who would later elect her as their tenant president. She would live there for the rest of her life. In 1986 though, she would win her biggest battle in Albany.

Rose Kryzak as a youngster in Russia (second from left)
with her brother Bill, sister Ida and mother Ann

Governor Mario Cuomo with Rose Kryzak

StateWide Senior Action Council Board of Directors, 1970's, Rose Kryzak on the far left with Executive Director Robert O'Donnell standing in back. President Rev. Howard Hills seated in middle

StateWide President Reverend Howard Hills of Rensselaer County honored by Governor Hugh Carey as New York State Senior Citizen of the Year. State Office for the Aging Director Lou Glasse and Senator Hugh Farley joined in the ceremony

Rally against Social Security cuts at Javits Federal Building,
New York City, late 1970's

Raphaela Muirhead congratulated by President Jimmy Carter for her service on StateWide's VISTA project in Bedford Stuyvesant, Brooklyn at VISTA's national meeting in Washington, 1980

Rose Kryzak speaking with Mike Burgess in the mid-1980's

50th anniversary celebration of Social Security at FDR Mansion in
Hyde Park. August 14, 1985, Sister Serena Branson, Executive
Director of Catholic Charities of Albany is at podium with (left to
right) Franklin D. Roosevelt, Jr., Governor Cuomo, Assemblyman
Denis Butler, Congressman Claude Pepper, New York State AFL-CIO
President Ed Cleary, and former HEW Secretary Arthur Flemming

Rose Kryzak with Assemblyman Paul Harenberg
and Senator Dean Skelos after receiving 1986 New York State
Senior Citizen of the Year Award from State Legislature

Rose Kryzak and StateWide members rally to pass prescription drug
bill under arch of State Capitol, June 1986

Governor Cuomo standing on a state trooper's desk outside his office on the second floor of the Capitol addressing seniors rallying to a pass prescription drug bill, December 10, 1986

Rose Kryzak and legislators watch Governor Cuomo sign the EPIC bill into law, December 1986 in Queens

StateWide staff and members with Assemblyman Paul Harenberg
rallying for Mandatory Medicare assignment legislation, 1988

Rose Kryzak, Bonnie Ray
and Mike Burgess at 1988 StateWide convention

Rose Kryzak keeps them laughing as she joins Senator Edward
Kennedy and others campaigning for David Dinkins
to be Mayor of New York City, 1989

CHAPTER NINE

AN *EPIC* BATTLE: THE FIGHT FOR PRESCRIPTION DRUG COVERAGE IN NEW YORK

T HE MANDATORY RETIREMENT BATTLE WHICH HAD PRE-OCCUPIED senior groups for years concluded and the focus was turned to enactment of a drug subsidy program. When Medicare was enacted in 1965 it did not include coverage for prescription drugs except for hospitalized patients. As the years passed though, drugs were used more often to treat illnesses and drug coverage became more important.

New Jersey and Pennsylvania had enacted prescription drug assistance programs by the early 1980's and advocacy organizations led by Citywide Advocates for Seniors in New York City developed model legislation patterned after the New Jersey program. In New York State, it wasn't a new idea either. As early as 1979, Governor Hugh Carey proposed a modest $10 million prescription subsidy program but it was so modest and inadequate that senior groups including StateWide rejected it in that form. Democrats in the Assembly drafted bills for such a program. Just two years earlier in 1977, the Legislature had passed a bill educating seniors about lower cost generic drugs and promoting their use. In the midst of many other issues like energy, Social Security and mandatory retirement, the deck had not been cleared to focus primarily on drug coverage as an issue as well as a movement.

During Mario Cuomo's campaign for Governor, he had pledged to support legislation to provide state subsidies for prescription drug coverage for seniors. Beginning in 1984, Citywide led by a charismatic Vito Lopez organized hundreds of seniors from senior citizen centers across New York City to come to Albany to demonstrate their power and lobby legislators on a platform of issues developed locally before the annual March trip. In March of 1984, Rose Kryzak served as a vice president with Citywide and delivered 30,000 petitions to state leaders calling for prescription drug coverage. By bringing over 1,500 persons to the convention center in the Empire State Plaza in Albany, Citywide was able to get the governor and top legislative leaders to address them. In his speech, Cuomo promised that before his first term was over he would present a plan for prescription drug coverage for needy seniors.

In August the following year, Cuomo appointed a special task force to look into the problem and come up with a proposal to meet his commitment. The task force was headed by Ilene Margolin, his chief human services advisor. However, the state bureaucracy had always de-emphasized aging legislation. Most of those in high positions in "human services" were veterans of public assistance programs. Their interests were in those programs. They viewed aging as a federal issue other than the state's role with long-term care supported by Medicaid.

However, Assembly Speaker Stanley Fink was so committed to the prescription drug issue he co-sponsored the Assembly bill with Paul Harenberg and let it be numbered A.1-a, meaning Assembly bill No 1-amended. The Assembly legislation modeled the New Jersey plan as Citywide had proposed. Seniors would pay a $10 fee to join the program and then $3 for each prescription. The Senate had proposed a more modest program that required seniors to pay more for coverage and would take effect after a deductible had been met. The Cuomo task force eventually came forward with a $38 million proposal for catastrophic coverage for seniors with high drug costs. Senior advocates and state legislators immediately criticized it because it was a far cry from the more widely available Assembly plan and even the Republican Senate plan was more generous.

Meanwhile, StateWide and other advocacy groups joined Citywide to make the issue its top priority in 1985 following passage of the mandatory retirement bill. When Citywide returned again with 1500 seniors in the winter of 1985, Rose Kryzak's job was to speak and then introduce Governor Cuomo. She read from her prepared remarks reminding the huge crowd of Cuomo's promise the year before and saying that everybody was still waiting. "How deep do the elderly have to sink in poverty before they can get help?" Rose asked. Recalling Cuomo's past promise of enacting a drug program, she observed, "Now in 1985 we are low in spirit." Cuomo got impatient at Rose's needling and decided to get up before she finished with her prepared remarks.

He knew how to handle Rose with humor. He said, "I only made two promises in my life, one to Matilda (his wife) and the other to Rose. So far, she is making me pay more for it." Then, he accepted the challenge and chided the group, wondering why it was so concerned with prescription drugs rather than with the plight of the very poor elderly on SSI who hadn't had a raise in their state supplement in years. He was trying to distract the group. He neglected to say that he hadn't proposed one either the previous year. He said they would get a prescription drug program and the crowd broke out into shouts of, "When, when, when?" Cuomo voiced one concern which may have played a role in the foot dragging on the bill. He said that when a bill was passed, he was sure conservatives would say it added to the state's reputation under him of being a "neo-Socialist state." That phrase had been used at the time in criticism of Cuomo by Patrick Buchanan who was the Communications Director for President Reagan.

The media loved the show that day and Dave Hepp of public television's *Inside Albany* would comment after his report on the event, "Has Mario Cuomo finally met his match from an 86-year old woman who knows how to use the media?" In an interview with Hepp, Rose rejected Cuomo's efforts to pit the needs of some groups against others. She said they all had to make their own way to the governor. She enchanted reporters reciting old jokes like she couldn't wait any longer for a prescription drug program because "I am so old I don't even buy green bananas." And, in vintage Kryzak form, she announced she would keep state leaders' feet to the fire:

"They (state leaders) haven't heard the last of me nor will they, nor should they. I'm 86 but I expect to be alive for a long time. I'm taking very good care of my health and as long as I am alive I'll be here every year to ask for what the people need."

Rose continued to differ with the governor. She was very good at picking up on themes used by politicians. She called on Cuomo to propose a "sound" prescription drug program, recalling his keynote address in San Francisco when he said, "Don't make speeches that sound good, make programs that are good and sound." Referring to the governor's theme of family, she said that there is a "little disagreement" in the family about prescription drugs now, but that it would be discussed and "worked out as it should be in a family."

The prescription drug bill was not without its critics. The Senate didn't want to subsidize "first dollar drugs." The State Division of the Budget under the governor's control worried about the explosive cost. In those days before welfare reform, there was still a strong sense that the state and nation shouldn't approve any more social welfare entitlement programs. The media also expressed concern about the cost of a drug subsidy program. As the battle intensified and the program seemed more likely to be enacted, the media and critics warned of a budget-busting program that would cost a half a billion dollars in a few years.

Demonstrations and rallies were held in Albany by hundreds of seniors who came wearing pill bottle necklaces. In the spring of 1985, the Assembly and then the Senate a few weeks later passed their own versions of a prescription drug bill. The Assembly passed its comprehensive bill and the Senate passed Senator Farley's bill which required seniors to first spend five percent of their income before getting any assistance. Neither side compromised and the session ended without any prescription drug program enacted.

The Legislature did pass an increase in the state supplement to the SSI program which Cuomo had proposed. He had been hounded by advocates on this issue too with Suleika Cabrera Drinane, Executive Director of the Institute for Puerto Rican and Hispanic Elderly giving him forty pounds of peanuts after he spoke at an Hispanic conference to signify how SSI recipients were tired of being given peanuts to live on.

Negotiations on the drug bill dragged on during the year. In December 1985, StateWide and other senior organizations issued a critical press release urging the governor "to get off the sidelines" and work aggressively to get a bill passed. StateWide had requested a meeting with Ilene Margolin, Cuomo's human services adviser but never got one. StateWide then requested to meet with the Governor himself. Finally, that meeting occurred in December 1985 but it was broadened to include a whole host of advocacy groups to discuss many issues of concern to seniors.

Early in 1986, which was an election year for the governor and state legislators, Cuomo and the Assembly united behind one bill with the Senate holding out for its own approach. More busloads of seniors had come in February for Citywide's annual trip and a rally was held with a march around the back side of the Capitol in June. Rose Kryzak's high profile advocacy for prescription drugs led to her selection as the Senior Citizen of the Year by Assemblyman Paul Harenberg and the State Legislature in 1986. On the first Tuesday of May which was always Senior Citizens Day, Rose's two children, Ann and Tommy, joined her in Albany for the award ceremony before several hundred persons in the Legislative Office Building which was also attended by Governor Cuomo and many legislators.

As the legislative session wound down in late June, there was real hope that a compromise would finally be reached. Senate and Assembly staffers said they were near agreement on the structure and eligibility guidelines for the program but there was an intractable disagreement over an item in the Democratic bill that required a change in the prescription pad for all consumers in the state. This change would give preference to generic drugs unless a doctor specifically wrote otherwise. It was to become StateWide's first big battle with the pharmaceutical companies which opposed the entire bill because of this generic provision.

The Senate insisted on removing the provision, saying the state shouldn't interfere with doctor's decisions. The Democrats wanted to control the cost of the program by using more generics however they were also responding to other consumer groups which had been promoting cheaper generic drugs. One drug company, Pfizer, went so far as to enlist a conservative seniors group based in Virginia which always seemed to side with the industry. They sent letters to all legislators opposing the prescription pad change. Statewide immediately noted that the letter, though on the group's stationery, was faxed from Pfizer headquarters.

Negotiations continued and we fully expected that before the Legislature left for the summer a drug bill would be passed. In fact, Rose Kryzak was very upset about what she heard might pass, a program that would require quarterly premiums and a twenty-five percent co-payment. She thought that seniors wouldn't find the program worth the bother. The last week of the session was exasperating and disheartening even if exciting. The battle to enact a drug bill ended at 4:00 a.m. on Thursday, July 3. After struggling all night to get a compromise, senior advocates were dispatched by Assembly negotiators to tell Senator Skelos, the new Chair of the Aging Committee, to ask Senate Majority Leader Warren Anderson to re-consider a final bill put together by the Assembly and the governor's office. Since Anderson had already said no, we thought the battle was over. The bill's death was confirmed at the grand staircase in the middle of the old building. There was Mario Cuomo with his coat and hat leaving with two others for home in the quiet and darkness of the hallway. With him gone, it was over. Negotiations had finally broken down and the legislators left for the summer. Rather than be dejected, we quickly realized that the failure to enact a bill was even better for the our campaign. The legislators were so embarrassed that a bill wasn't passed as they had so often promised that they seemed almost certain to return during the summer for that purpose. We expected a great deal of media coverage to be focused just on this one issue.

It seemed that Cuomo was especially uncomfortable about his promise. He wanted the legislators to return in the summer. He called Senator Skelos on the golf course to tell him he wanted his assistance getting the bill passed in the Senate. Ilene Margolin called me frequently, giving me updates on where things stood from her perspective.

StateWide and other senior advocacy organization staff met in New York on July 10 to discuss strategy. It was a very lively and somewhat testy meeting, but finally there was general agreement that the group preferred the bill drafted by the Assembly and the governor's office.

On July 14th, a disappointed Rose Kryzak sent a letter to Cuomo signed by ten organizations asking him to call a special session of the Legislature:

"We were solemnly promised a bill, the Assembly unanimously adopted a bill we supported but the Senate leadership callously ignored the needs of the poor. Now many senior citizens will have to make the bitter choice between medicine and food...The immense prestige and leadership of the governor's office must be used in a determined drive for the passage of an affordable prescription drug (program) as has been done for other legislation."

During July, Cuomo and Fink wanted to continue working toward a deal. Some weren't happy that we were compromising from our original proposal. Fink wanted to meet with all the advocates for the bill and we met him in New York on July 17. He brought a dose of reality into the discussions as he said he had agreed to spend $125 million and he wanted our views on how the program should be structured rather than talk about our ideal bill. After the meeting with Fink, Cuomo decided he would sign any bill that cost no more than $125 million, that had an inflation factor, a sunset clause and that promoted generic drugs by changing the prescription pad. He also started the three-way negotiations with the Assembly and the Senate again. He wanted a tentative, negotiated agreement before a special session of the Legislature was called. It was still expected that it could happen in August. It didn't.

Discussions dragged on. Finally, the governor and the Assembly agreed on a new bill and Cuomo and Fink invited us all to join them on September 10th at Cuomo's office in the World Trade Center to announce the proposal. Rose and I sat in front of Cuomo and Fink who were at the head of an "I" shaped table arrangement. We met to discuss the bill before the press conference. Like other events I had seen him at, Cuomo seemed uptight at first, almost defensive, as if expecting us to be hostile. He opened the meeting and again lectured us about the needs of the poor and said SSI recipients deserved state money before a prescription drug bill was funded. With that out of his system, he grew more relaxed as the discussion began with our representatives led by Rose. She and Cuomo again started joking. He said he wanted her to speak to the press first, so he'd know what she had said. He really did want it that way and she went first.

The reporters listened to statements by Rose, Cuomo, Fink and Harry Felder of AARP. Then, they started questioning what the Senate's reaction would be and what we would do if they were unmoved. Harry Felder said the AARP would use "all of its resources." The governor didn't like the line of questioning, so he stepped up and suggested that he didn't expect them to be intransigent and they should be given a chance to respond.

I was not optimistic about the response. I felt like we were back to the end of the session. Both sides were locked in to very different positions. Only if the leaders had the will to pull it off did I think the bill would be passed.

We were scheduled to meet with Phil Pinsky, Senator Anderson's top staff person on this issue. We felt the Assembly had put us in a bad position. They were pressuring us to go after the Senate and get them to support the new bill. Fink kept saying it was our bill and he couldn't compromise further because we wouldn't accept it. It was true, we had already backed off our original plan. We knew this was the last phase of the battle. The bill must pass in the next few weeks in a special session or its momentum and chances for passage after the election would recede. If no progress was made in the negotiations the governor might not be committed enough to take a chance and call the legislators back to pass it. Advocates were frustrated by this turn of events.

Even though the issue dragged on through the summer and fall of 1986, we felt comfortable the issue would be resolved in a special session whenever the legislators were called back to town. We shouldn't have been. Many lobbyists and persons involved in state government were skeptical after the long wait, but negotiations seemed to be continuing. In fact, the negotiators for the Senate, Assembly and governor had made substantial progress. They had finally reached an agreement on the major programmatic issues of the bill regarding income, eligibility and benefit levels. This agreement was no small achievement. After years of arguing whether the program should be targeted toward lower-income seniors as an income transfer program as the Assembly wanted or an insurance-type program for lower and middle income seniors as the Senate wanted, they had basically agreed to combine the two approaches and spend more money to placate both sides. That was the Albany way: rather than split differences, add them.

Governor Cuomo won a record re-election victory in November. His sixty-five percent of the vote was the highest total ever received in a gubernatorial election. Even Governor Rockefeller hadn't done that. As December began, the only major outstanding issue was the generic design of the prescription pad. The Senate Republicans had long ago agreed to accept a one-line pad which was automatically for generic drugs unless the doctor specified a brand name. They felt that was their major concession. In return, they wanted to have a box for the doctor to put his or her initials to designate the brand name. The Assembly and the generic drug lobby claimed such a move would make it almost as easy as the current pad to prescribe brand names.

Despite this disagreement, it seemed that there was plenty of room for further compromise as all sides discussed different sizes and shapes for the box and using initials instead of the doctor's, such as d.a.w., "dispense as written," to designate the brand name. With the prospect of the Legislature returning soon, many felt that would be the impetus to finally get the issue resolved.

On Wednesday, December 3, 1986 all that changed. A special session of the Legislature was called by Governor Cuomo for December 10 but he was not putting the drug bill on the agenda. Despite everything said to us, this was not a "must do" on the agenda. The negotiations had become deadlocked. No further meetings or compromises were available. It seemed, for the first time, that the bill was doomed. It would not pass unless something dramatic changed the circumstances. Ilene Margolin then confirmed the deadlock.

We couldn't believe that the legislators and the governor could actually let the bill and the issue and our hopes just fade and die. There was anger at Cuomo for making the promise to the seniors and then not fighting hard enough for it. Sure, his staff was negotiating and working hard and couldn't make everybody agree. However, senior groups felt that Cuomo wasn't using the power he had to pressure for an agreement. At the same time, the governor was telling reporters that the issue would be put on the agenda at the special session if an agreement could be reached. He was not committing to fight for it. He wasn't saying he wanted the agreement and would fight for it.

So, when I spoke to Ilene Margolin that afternoon, I deliberately told her that, while we had become friends through the many months of working on the issue, it would be necessary for the coming week to react professionally. I meant she should not take it personally what we were going to do. I didn't want to hurt her because I felt she had worked very hard and sincerely to get an agreement.

Stunned, Ilene wanted to know what I was getting at. "Are you going to attack the governor?" she demanded to know. I said we were and she got very agitated and said it was unfair, that she had tried everything to get an agreement. I said the governor made a promise and we, as senior advocates, had to stand up and still fight to get the bill passed. After listening, Ilene was more composed and said she understood, but was just frustrated by it all.

In fact, I had already called the reporters for the Albany newspapers and told them that the negotiations were collapsing and attacked the governor. Lise Bang-Jensen of the Albany's *Knickerbocker News* then called Rose Kryzak in Queens who said, "We're not going to sit around like a bunch of clay pigeons waiting to get picked off!" That quote and my remarks about the Governor making promises were in the morning paper. They didn't sit well with the governor's office but I didn't hear anything because I was in New York meeting with senior organizations and other groups regarding health care. At the end of that meeting, I told the others about the collapse of the negotiations and began planning a rally for the following week. We asked the other groups to begin sending postcards to their legislators.

When I returned to the office on Friday, I was ready for the battle to begin. I dropped by the press room at the Capitol and spoke to a couple reporters. I told a few of them I wanted to talk about how the seniors had been sold down the river by the governor and the Legislature. I wanted to broaden the attack and said that if the drug bill didn't pass, Cuomo's record for senior citizens would be lousy. I said this especially because, we were continually told that no other major spending could be undertaken for the elderly since the drug bill would cost so much. If the drug bill didn't pass, not only would it be lost, but so would other possible initiatives that were not advanced because of it. I explained to the reporters that we were going to insist on getting major increases in spending on other programs.

I left the press room enlightened and discouraged because all of the reporters had always doubted the bill would pass. Jeff Schmalz of the *New York Times* said he definitely wanted to get back to me and do a story about 'how the drug bill died." I felt badly when he said that Cuomo never wanted the bill in the first place. Schmalz who spent a lot of time with Cuomo said he was convinced that Cuomo would run for president and did not want to be tagged with enacting such a big social welfare program. Bennett Roth of the *Albany Times-Union* said the exact same thing. I had heard that conjectured before, but never so matter-of-factly or authoritatively.

On that frustrating Friday, I continued to regret what I thought was a major mistake. I had assumed the bill would be passed so we never built the grassroots pressure. Despite the advice of a trusted senior advocate in Washington, to really put the heat on during the election campaign, we never did. It wasn't that I didn't want to. Rather, it was a big undertaking to coordinate activity in all the campaigns and we didn't have the staff or funds for what seemed like a sure thing. Now, I wished I had all that time back, six more weeks to organize. Instead we had only one. I resolved to try to make up for it and undertake an all-out effort to reach Senators. I didn't have close relationships with many Senate Republicans which made the task difficult. They never seemed to be influenced by us. They seemed more influenced by industry and providers and talked about all the reasons for their position. That day, I decided to call Senator Stafford of Plattsburgh who I could talk with and who was very interested in the issue. He didn't return my call at that time.

I also tried to reach Phil Pinsky, the Senate Counsel who was their negotiator. We had always been polite on the phone before, but this time, we got testy and began raising our voices. He said we always blamed the Senate and the governor and never attacked the Assembly even though they refused to budge. I then said that the Senate couldn't have it both ways, telling us not to make the issue partisan during the campaign and then saying it was so quiet during the campaign that the Senators didn't feel the seniors were demanding the bill. Finally, we calmed down. Phil explained his concerns about generics, citing doctors' opinions. I asked him not to give up and implored him to resolve the issue. He said he would keep trying to get an agreement.

We thought about how to devise a spectacular rally that would create such an uproar that the situation could be turned around. We decided we would need placards and we should sing patriotic songs.

On Sunday morning, Ilene Margolin called me at home. I hadn't spoken with her since the story was in the newspapers quoting me criticizing the governor for not keeping his promise. Ilene was very conciliatory and said that, she could understand why we were so upset because the press reported the Governor hadn't put the bill on the agenda for the special session. She said he had planned to all along, but somehow he hadn't presented it as clearly as he should have. She told me the agenda would be formally announced soon.

I felt good about her call. It seemed the governor's people were concerned about the issue and wanted to try to avoid any further public attacks in the press and other confrontations that could come with our rally. I told Ilene we were dead serious about it and would do whatever was necessary to get the bill passed. I told her that we were planning actions that would throw the other issues in the special session such as New York City transit financing off the front page of every paper in the state. Ilene wanted the bill to pass, so even if she didn't agree with our tactics she understood our role as advocates and organizers.

As the week began, it was like we were in the midst of a political campaign, because it would take that kind of organization and effort to win. The passage of the bill was still unlikely but that, at least, we had achieved our first step, getting the bill on the agenda. Now, the bill would officially have to be addressed by the legislators. Even if they did nothing, they had to go on the record as ignoring the bill.

Despite what any of the other political professionals and media thought, there were still four major factors in favor of the bill's chances of passage. First, was the leadership of an 86-year-old woman, Rose Kryzak, and her ability to use the press. Second, there were only four items on the agenda and one had already been resolved regarding extra judges to handle drug cases. We also were certain to get extensive media coverage and I knew how legislators and the governor were so concerned about that. Finally, we had the drama of Mario Cuomo, the hottest presidential prospect in America under the gun for not keeping a major public promise to senior citizens. It was a potent formula for winning in my mind.

I had decided that I would spend all day Monday on the phone, calling all the activists we had all over the state and simply urging them to call their State Senator to urge that something be done about the drug bill. I focused on the upstate districts, because we were stronger there. I tried to call someone who was a senior leader in every Senate district. In some areas we had leaders in every county to help.

I simply told all of them that the bill was going to die and they had to help. I gave them their legislator's phone number at the district office and told them to get as many people as possible to call. I didn't want any senators to say they hadn't heard much from their senior constituents. So many calls and visits were made to Senator Ronald Stafford's office in Plattsburgh, he called me and said he got the message but that he was a supporter because his district was poor. He vaguely stated that we should focus on some other senators in other parts of the state, giving some geographic regions rather than names.

Throughout the day, I continued to talk with the leaders of other senior organizations, planning the rally and assisting to organize the buses. The New York City people said they would have five buses. Binghamton would bring one. A van was coming from Monticello and we would round up whomever we could from the Capital District. We didn't need the huge crowds of 1500 which came from New York before. A big crowd would be too unwieldy. We just needed enough people to make a dramatic showing.

We decided to try to keep our side of the issue in the press to keep the pressure up. We issued a press release each day. On Monday, we simply announced that Rose Kryzak would be leading the march and gave some details of where it would start and some vague reference about appearing in the Senate galleries.

I got Tuesday's press release earlier. I also had to take part in another press conference announcing our campaign with other groups to get the state to provide health coverage through Medicaid for those who didn't have any insurance. I learned that the governor was also holding a press conference at the same time. So, I knew we wouldn't get any coverage with competition from him. I went up to the press room to drop off our press release on the drug bill and spent some time urging the reporters to ask the governor about the status of the bill.

After our press conference, I went back to the Blue Room in the Capitol where Cuomo had his events. After his announcement of a new Director of the State Police, he opened the floor to the reporters' questions. They wanted to talk about the special session. The governor gave the overview of the three remaining issues and outlined their status as he saw it. When he came to the drug bill, he simply and matter-of-factly said that negotiations had ended and unless something changed, they were not expected to resume. The reporters asked if he realized that representatives of the seniors were in the room and that they were coming to Albany on Thursday to protest and keep pushing legislators to act. Cuomo seemed a little surprised. Apparently, he was only beginning to realize that he would have to deal with Rose and hundreds of seniors in less than 48 hours.

After Cuomo's press conference, the *Associated Press* wrote a story saying Cuomo had called the drug bill dead. Later that day, Ilene Margolin who was obviously worried about our reaction, called to say that the Governor wanted to meet with Rose and went so far as to suggest that she meet him after a literary reception the next day. It now seemed that Cuomo wanted the press to see him meeting with Rose. What a great breakthrough we thought this was. It would take forever for him to escort the slow-walking

Rose through the vast underground Concourse of the Empire State Plaza back to his office in the State Capitol.

Rose arrived on the bus on Wednesday morning for our press conference that morning. My friend, Artie Malkin, a lobbyist for the generic drug industry had printed twelve pages of computer paper, detailing over $80,000 in campaign contributions from drug companies in recent years in Albany. I got up and rolled out the paper which spanned eleven feet. A mob of reporters showed up and the roll of paper really caught their attention.

Rose also had an idea to ask the governor for his mother's telephone number. She thought that would be a funny way to startle him. I told her to make sure to do it when the press was around. So, we planned that she would say that when the literary reception was over and the governor met her as the press trailed. So, startle him she did. When she asked him, a United Press International photographer snapped a famous picture of Rose badgering Cuomo as he put his palm to his forehead and said, "You and my mother would create an empire."

When we made it back to Cuomo's office, he invited our group into a small conference room. Bonnie Ray of StateWide's staff was with Rose and me along with three of StateWide's most active local members, seniors Michael and Ann Widzowski from Cohoes and Reverend John Edmond, StateWide's long-time legislative Chairman from Rensselaer County. Cuomo listened to our concerns about passing the EPIC (Elderly Pharmaceutical Insurance Coverage) bill and we discussed the generics issue. I told him that one senator had bad mouthed generic drugs saying that some of these generics could have been "made in a bathtub in Mexico." Cuomo agreed that he would try to get a deal with the Assembly and Senate. He concluded by telling us that he would be meeting with Fink and Anderson in the morning and that we should come by while we were demonstrating and wait outside and he would emerge and update us on their negotiations.

On Thursday morning, we woke up to find the front page of the now-defunct *Knickerbocker News* with a picture of Rose that took up half of the top half of the page "above the fold" as they say in the business. An accompanying article described the coming rally and the arrival back in town of the Legislature for the special session. In the far right hand column of the paper was a front page article about the on-going story of the Iran-contra affair with a picture of John Poindexter, a top aide to President Reagan who faced possible indictment. We joked that Rose's picture dwarfed that of Poindexter.

Protest rallies and demonstrations were always a sensitive point for some seniors active in StateWide. Many in New York City were used to rallies, having been more active in unions. For upstate and rural seniors though, they were not used to this more strident activism. By December though, they began to realize the benefits of such protesting because other methods had not succeeded in getting a bill passed.

Buses arrived from New York City and downstate with over 200 seniors, prepared as if going into a decisive battle to win a war. We had placards printed saying, "We don't have PACs (political action committees) to pay off Senators." Some were armed with homemade signs as well.

They entered the Capitol up the escalator from the underground concourse and from there walked to the Governor's office on the second floor. We began a chorus of "God Bless America" and then stopped in front of Cuomo's office where a pack of reporters waited in the hallway while he met with Speaker Fink and Senator Anderson. We needed to keep busy rather than stand around so we found a chair for Rose to stand on and be seen by the crowd while she gave a speech.

After a while Cuomo came out and he tried to address the crowd as he promised the night before. The crowd couldn't see him and finally he jumped on top of the state trooper's desk in the hallway. He told them what had transpired in the negotiations and discussed what the problems were. He said that generics "weren't made in a bathtub in Mexico" as some Republicans were saying. However, he said he couldn't put a gun to the head of the Senate Republicans. Upset with that remark, Lillian Kandell, a heavy-set woman representing JPAC bellowed, "I came up here in 18 inches of snow (last February) and you promised." If you won't pull the trigger, we'll get somebody else to." He told them to go see Senator Warren Anderson, the Majority Leader. A smaller group had gone up and laid siege to Anderson's office and his aide, Bob Reed, who said some staffpersons would meet with the group if they went to a first floor conference room. The group refused saying they wanted to see Anderson.

Finally, after seeing Cuomo who urged them to go after Senate Republicans, the group went down to the first floor meeting room and Anderson appeared. He raised concerns about generic drugs which Bill Michalski, StateWide's president, attacked, asking Anderson if he was smarter than the FDA which approved the drugs. Anderson voiced concerns raised by some doctors but he finally said he was open to looking again at the issue.

Just as we had expected, the rally and the media attention completely changed the situation. Cuomo indicated that he had asked Ilene Margolin to return to Albany from a New York City meeting and to contact her legislative counterparts, Doug McCuen from the Assembly and Phil Pinsky from the Senate, to immediately begin negotiations. It didn't matter anymore. We knew after the rally we had won, especially after reading the morning papers. There were photos of the demonstrations in papers all over the state. The *New York Times* and the *Associated Press* had photos of Cuomo standing on the desk in the hall. The *Schenectady Gazette* headlined its story, "Elderly Besiege Capitol Seeking Drug Subsidies." The *Knickerbocker News* headlined, "Angry crowd confronts governor, blames him for drug plan failure" and quoted Ed Pomeroy with Citizen Action's Binghamton chapter saying, "I wouldn't mind being arrested. At 73 years of age, I don't think it's too late to get started."

Most satisfying was Jeff Schmalz report in the New York Times. Rather than writing about the demise of the bill, he reported,

"hundreds of elderly people held demonstrations in the hall-ways, singing 'God Bless America' and calling for passage of prescription drug subsidies. The Democratic Governor, emerging from his second floor office, was swept along in a sea of elderly people wanting to know why no such plan had been enacted. He finally climbed atop a desk, shouting to be heard, and blamed the failure on Republicans, who control the State Senate."

The negotiations continued. One week later, the State Legislature ended its special session and passed the Elderly Pharmaceutical Insurance Coverage (EPIC) program. Jeff Schmalz report of the bill's passage ran on the front page of the *New York Times* on December 17, "A new state program to subsidize prescription drug purchases for up to 1.2 million elderly people was tentatively agreed to tonight by Governor Cuomo and key lawmakers after one of the longest and most emotional political battles of Mr. Cuomo's term in office."

Two weeks later at a senior center in Queens, Mario Cuomo signed the bill into law with Rose Kryzak next to him and the bill's legislative sponsors nearby and Lillian Kandell in the audience. Rose Kryzak had become an icon and a legend to the seniors in New York State who would come to call her the "the mother of the EPIC program." And, she got a letter from Dr. Eugene Callender, Director of the State Office for the Aging in which he said,

> *"There are very few significant events that take place in history that can be attributed to the work of any one human being. But I can honestly say that we would not have Prescription Drug Subsidy Program in New York State without a Rose Kryzak. Congratulations and thank you."*

The passage of EPIC was controversial among many seniors especially in New York City. Vito Lopez of Citywide Advocates rejected the final bill, feeling disillusioned that it had been so watered down from the original proposal. He criticized StateWide and others for negotiating the deal and approving it with the governor's office. Though Rose Kryzak was never one for compromises, she also knew a victory when she saw one. She was involved up close and had been there dealing with Cuomo. With EPIC she was willing to accept less than the original bill because she had seen first-hand that it was the best that could be achieved and that it was a major gain for her peers. She always noted that it was such a big victory it couldn't be rejected and she was pragmatic, believing that, by getting a foot in the door, changes and improvements could be made later and she was right.

That became necessary because in the early years of the program, the enthusiasm and enrollment in New York City were low. Many seniors found all the co-payments, premiums and deductibles too confusing and too expensive. Within a couple years there were calls to change the program with Assembly members pushing reforms which were closer to the original bill. The foot was in the door though as Rose said. Commenting on the EPIC victory just months earlier, she said, "Sometimes even one person can make a difference. The lesson of that campaign is if you make up your mind and keep to your goal, advocacy works."

In October of 1987, the EPIC program began with Grace Keelan of Suffolk County on Long Island becoming the program's first enrollee. Rose was named to be on an advisory board for the program and she dutifully attended every meeting.

In that summer of 1987, I invited Rose to join my family for a vacation in the Adirondacks. She had loved the mountains and for many years, she and Kay would rent a housekeeping cabin on Lake George. They loved canoeing and swimming. Other members of the family would often drive up to join them. She would yell, "Throw me a donut," referring to an intertube, noted her niece Lucy Zaslow.

My son, Joseph had just been born in April 1987 and we rented a cabin in Ray Brook, between Saranac Lake and Lake Placid. We rented another one for my mother and Rose. Rose loved being back in the mountains for the first time since Kay's death. We spent a wonderful week and she regaled us with stories of her long life. She would become a surrogate "great grandmother" for my kids and they called her G.G. Rose.

CHAPTER TEN

GREEDY GEEZERS, GREEDY DOCTORS AND PATIENTS RIGHTS

IN THE LATE 1980's, THE ISSUE OF PRESCRIPTION DRUG COVERAGE, which had become such a focus of state attention became a national concern as momentum built for including drug coverage in Medicare. Though the nation still had huge annual deficits in the late 1980's, Democrats who controlled Congress looked for a way to provide the coverage. They came up with a proposal that was self-financed with Medicare beneficiaries paying for the entire benefit, a move that many later felt was a huge mistake. This provision was passed as part of a Medicare catastrophic coverage bill that included caps on spending for hospital care and other services. To finance the drug coverage, an additional mandatory premium would have to be paid by all Medicare beneficiaries on a sliding income scale basis. For more affluent seniors, it ended up costing several hundred dollars a year even if they already had coverage from a supplemental insurance plan from their private employer or even if they didn't need the coverage.

When the financial impact of the new coverage became apparent, more affluent seniors rebelled and demanded that the new law be repealed. In a famous scene, they swarmed with anger around the car of Congressman Dan Rostenkowski in Chicago, then the powerful Chairman of the Ways and Means Committee. The pressure was so great that the law was repealed.

StateWide had not played an active role in supporting the measure, but the expanded coverage especially helped lower-income seniors. The financing though, an income transfer from more affluent seniors to those who were lower-income, was not the best approach. Many senior advocates felt it should have been financed through the regular Medicare payroll tax paid by the entire working population. It was an agreement reached by Washington senior advocacy groups who obviously didn't expect the reaction from some seniors. They felt it was the best deal they could get in the climate of massive federal deficits so they took it. Unlike our EPIC compromise though this one imposed mandatory cost increases.

Helen Quirini, who was then President of the Schenectady County Council of Senior Citizens organized local efforts to repeal it. "The new law is a costly measure with modest benefits which will put an extraordinary financial burden on elder Medicare recipients," she wrote in a pamphlet.

Rose and other seniors were very concerned about the political fallout from the repeal of the catastrophic bill. In Washington, the AARP and other senior advocates were told by Congressional leaders that it would be years before they took up a major senior health issue again because of how they were burned by the catastrophic bill. More and more in the media, the phrase "greedy geezers" kept being used to describe seniors, a far cry from a decade earlier when the poverty of seniors was a source of national concern. Meeting at JPAC in New York City in 1989, Rose and others discussed how they could counteract what they felt was an unfair criticism. Getting their children and grandchildren to take up their cause by writing letters supporting the needs of their parents was discussed and everyone agreed it was a good idea.

Patients' Rights

In the mid and late 1980's, StateWide also became concerned about new Medicare financing policies that changed the way payments were made to hospitals. Medicare beneficiaries and senior advocates feared that the introduction of "DRGs" or diagnostic-related groups as a basis of payment would result in older people being discharged from hospitals "quicker and sicker." The DRGs were simply the classification of hundreds of diagnoses with a set payment attached to them. The DRG was to be an average that would encourage hospitals to treat patients in the number of days that were recommended or even try to discharge patients in less than the average number of days and thereby save money. It was supposed to average out, some patients would be less expensive than average and others more expensive.

Seniors worried that hospitals would view the DRGs as maximums not averages. StateWide sought money from the State Legislature to monitor quality of care in hospitals for all patients not just older persons. A statewide toll-free "patients rights' hotline" was established. With this project StateWide began handling individual complaints and problems. I hired Bonnie Ray as the Project Coordinator. She had been active in social justice activities in the past working with the Job Corps in Mississippi in the tumultuous 1960's.

StateWide staff began to assist patients and their families to challenge hospital discharge decisions. Appeals were filed with Medicare and meetings were held with the state Department of Health to discuss patients' rights. The efforts of StateWide and other organizations led to a growing patients' rights movement that would bloom in the years to come as HMOs, (health maintenance organizations), continued efforts to cap payments and deny care that patients and their families felt their coverage provided whether it was Medicare or employer-paid insurance. Rose Kryzak liked the patients rights' initiative and she would later go under-cover with Lani Sanjek of StateWide's New York City office to determine if hospitals were informing patients of their rights. StateWide also worked closely with Dr. Cynthia Rudder, Executive Director of the Nursing Home Community Coalition of New York State, on patients rights in long-term facilities.

Earlier, in 1986, Rose had testified before the Hospital Review and Planning Council of the New York State Department of Health:

"Twenty years ago when Medicare became law, the elderly felt that their health problems had been solved. But what are the cruel realities? Now, the elderly pay more for health care out of pocket than they did before 1965. Is there a possibility that Medicare patients in New York State are now at risk of being still worse off - being discharged from hospitals sicker and quicker because of the new payment arrangements under DRGs?"

As StateWide president, Rose made a few trips around the state. She was invited by Kathleen Laramie, the energetic Director of the Clinton County Office for the Aging, to visit Plattsburgh, just south of the Canadian border. There at the D'Youville Senior Center in June 1987 she delivered to seniors and the media remarks that had become her standard for her fourteen years in senior advocacy. She lamented again that the United States stood alone with South Africa as the only industrialized countries without national health insurance. She added that seniors should not suffer anymore from President Reagan's budget cuts. "The elderly should not be called on to make any more sacrifices to reduce the deficit," which she said was caused by tax reductions and military spending, "the gains of the greedy" not the "pains of the needy." It was vintage Kryzak.

As president of StateWide in 1987-1988, Rose wrote a column in StateWide's *Senior Action* bi-monthly newspaper and she chose to focus on many different topics. She researched them. She always was cutting articles out of the *New York Times* and making copies. After her studying, Rose wrote carefully drafted articles advocating for improvements in programs for seniors. In the August-September 1987 issue she discussed cuts in federal housing and quoted the 1980 federal census about the number of units lacking central heating and complete plumbing. She argued that, "Decent, safe and sanitary shelter are the bare necessities of life," and concluded, "the federal government must reverse its priorities and build houses instead of bombs" It was another shot against the Reagan Administration.

In September of 1987 as Rose's term as president came to an end, I decided to leave StateWide. I had been recruited by the human services coalition, SENSES, (Statewide Network for Social and Economic Security) to become their Executive Director, and I accepted. It was a hard decision and it was not easy saying goodbye. I had been thinking of trying to find a job that had a broader focus than senior citizens. SENSES touched on many issue areas. In April of that year, our first child, Joseph was born and my wife was on maternity leave. SENSES offered a substantial pay raise. That sounded especially great to me. Bonnie Ray was selected by the Board to replace me. I was going to be only a couple blocks away and, of course, I kept in touch with Rose and Bonnie.

I learned quickly though that I had made a mistake and should have stayed at StateWide. I spent two unhappy years at SENSES and then moved on to the Non-Profit Resource Center, providing training and information about state government to mostly smaller non-profit groups.

In February 1988, Citywide made its annual pilgrimage to Albany with 1350 persons again filling the Convention Center in the Empire State Plaza. The *New York Times* did a feature story on the trip, "Young at Heart Politically, Elderly Lobby" which began: "At 4 feet 10 inches Rose Kryzak could not be easily seen from her place behind the podium in the Convention Hall. But as she spoke in a reasoned and determined way about the needs of the elderly, she sure could be heard." When a director of a senior center greeted her by saying, "It's superlady," Rose responded in her typical way, "What superlady?" I can't see, I can't hear, I can't walk."

Later that year, Governor Cuomo sent her one of many honorary citations she received from him. In it, he included a quote from Aristotle about old age:

"Friends are an aid to the young to guard them from error: to the elderly to attend to their wants and to supplement their failing powers of action: to those in the prime of life to assist them to noble deeds.'

She liked Aristotle but preferred Cicero! She sent him a letter on October 4th:

"Thank you for the citation you sent me on the occasion of New York StateWide Senior Action Council's tribute to me. I particularly like the quote from Aristotle. I want you to have a quote from a thinker of another country, Cicero, that I advocate by:
'Old age is honored on the condition that it defends itself, maintains its rights, is subservient to no one, and to the last breath rules over its own domain'."

Anybody who knew Rose appreciated her passion, her intellect, her energy and her sense of humor. After Kay's death she still traveled and announced "I am going on vacation for my 89th birthday. I am going to Greece. That's not the best part. I am taking a young man with me. He's a younger man. - 86. Later she joked, "He was good, but for his age, he wasn't as good as I was hoping."

In 1988, Governor Cuomo again was pleased to sign another increase in the state's payment for SSI recipients. He had proposed the increase and made special mention of it on Senior Citizen's Day that year. Many had thought Cuomo might run for President in 1988, but he bowed out of the running though he was believed to have a great shot at winning the nomination. His refusal to run enabled a neighboring ethnic Governor, Michael Dukakis of Massachusetts to win the Democratic nomination The big senior issue in New York, also came from Massachusetts.

Even before the EPIC battle was finished, Rose and StateWide had another issue in mind for an advocacy campaign: Medicare overcharges by doctors. Assemblyman Harenberg liked to note Rose's persistence by indicating how she wanted to raise the issue of doctor payments to follow up the EPIC campaign. She had heard that senior organizations in other states had pushed legislation mandating that doctors take Medicare's payments as "payment in full" and not be able to overcharge seniors beyond Medicare's customary charges. Federal law allowed doctors who participated in the Medicare program to charge up to fifteen percent more than what Medicare paid. Most seniors were not aware that such limits existed. When they learned more about the issue, they argued that doctors should accept Medicare payments as a condition of participating in the program.

At the 1986 convention, even before EPIC was passed, Rose was ready to begin the fight for "Medicare assignment" because she had heard about the passage of the Massachusetts bill that year

"I'd like to talk about the Massachusetts plan we'd like to propose for New York... What I am telling you, after this convention, one of our major campaigns will be getting the State Assembly to introduce a bill in the State of New York, that what Massachusetts can do, the State of New York can do better. And, we are going to be calling on you to get to all of your legislators to get to work on the plan we propose."

So, Assemblyman Harenberg drafted a bill which had Assemblymen Richard Gottfried and Ed Sullivan of Manhattan as co-prime sponsors. Governor Cuomo introduced his own bill. In the Senate, Democrat George Onorato of Queens introduced the Harenberg bill but there was no enthusiasm for it among the majority Senate Republicans. In October 1987, public hearings were held in four cities. At the Buffalo hearing, staff for the State Office for the Aging suggested that Medicare assignment should be "means-tested." The testimony said that "consideration of income should be incorporated into the program, to ensure to the extent possible, that physicians may retain discretion regarding assignment acceptance for their more wealthy patients."

While that view may have seemed reasonable, means testing was anathema to senior advocates. In a rare break with SOFA, StateWide announced its opposition to SOFA's position on the front page of *Senior Action* newsletter. Rose expressed her disappointment and was quoted in the StateWide's paper saying, "The State Office for the Aging has taken a position on this issue which is totally contrary to the position of just about every senior citizen advocacy group across the state."

The disagreement with SOFA showed that it was not going to be an easy battle. It turned into a four-year legislative battle pitting the seniors against the powerful State Medical Society. The doctors' lobby was adamantly opposed to the bill and was ready to use its resources and membership of 28,000 doctors in the state to fight it. Over 70 members of the Democratic-controlled Assembly became co-sponsors. There was unease though and Assemblyman Harenberg said at least one co-sponsor spoke against it in the party caucus. Some legislators didn't want to get involved in regulating a federal program. Others were listening to alarm bells from the State Medical Society saying doctors would leave the state.

StateWide and the united coalition of senior advocacy organizations decided to go all out for the bill like they had done to win the EPIC program. Advocates turned Senior Citizens Day, May 1, 1988 into a rally for Medicare assignment. A change in legislative leadership the year earlier didn't help. The senior's ally, Stanley Fink had retired and was succeeded by, Mel Miller of Brooklyn who didn't want to offend the doctors. Miller had less patience with the senior advocates and seemed more amused than impressed with Rose. When she came out after meeting with him for the first time after he became Speaker, she was disappointed and found him to be not someone she would trust to advocate for seniors. He was no Stanley Fink.

Rose's relationship with Mario Cuomo proved helpful though in dealing with Miller. Rose came to Albany to lobby in July. She didn't have an appointment with Cuomo but she wanted to go up to his office and try to see him anyway. Just as she got to the second floor near his office door, she saw him coming. He saw her and began taking off his coat in a comical gesture to suggest that he was ready to do battle with her. She told him that she wanted his help on the bill and he agreed. He told the press later, " I made it clear to the people on the Assembly side we're very eager to see this bill voted on."

Cuomo was relaxed and enjoyed seeing Rose. He invited her and the rest of us into his office and then gave a tour of the Red Room and the desk that Thomas E. Dewey used. Dewey was so short that he had a little platform to stand on and Cuomo urged Rose to do the same. Later that day, after the lobbying was done, Rose came to my house and rested. The phone rang. It was Michael Dowling of the Governor's staff. He said the Governor was coming on the line. I was stunned that he was calling my home. He told me he spoke with the Assembly leadership to push the bill.

The campaign intensified and by 1989, there were major efforts to have the bill passed in the Assembly. The State Medical Society had mounted an all-out attack on the legislation. It took full page ads in major newspapers saying doctors would leave the state and seniors would not get as much time with them. In 1989, they even broadened their effort into an attack on older people, raising the "greedy geezer" theme and saying seniors were selfish and weren't paying their fair share and they would be burdening younger people raising their cost of health care. StateWide and the other senior advocates responded in kind, attacking the greed of doctors who were unwilling to see their incomes slightly reduced. An outraged Bonnie Ray responded in StateWide's newspaper,

"It is outrageous that the Medical Society chooses to ignore the lifetime of hard work and financial contributions that seniors have made to the Social Security system that have earned them the right to health care. Seniors paid their insurance premiums when they young, just as younger people are paying now."

On Senior Citizens Day, May 2, 1989 an outdoor rally was held behind the Capitol and speakers argued that seniors in New York State had been overcharged $250 million in 1988 according to the Health Care Financing Administration. Seniors couldn't understand why the bill wasn't going to the floor for a vote it since they knew the bill had enough co-sponsors to pass. If a majority of members of the chamber were co-sponsors or publicly supported the bill, then it should have been passed. It wasn't that simple though and the bill never made it to the floor in 1989. Miller saw no need in an off-election year to have his members go on the record displeasing one side or the other.

It was different though in 1990. It was an election year, and it ended in a zero. In Albany that always meant it was a good year for organized citizens groups because legislators were not only running for re-election, but that a new census would lead to re-apportionment. In that environment, legislators were more likely than ever to pass a number of popular bills and programs which might have been long sought by advocates but never passed by both houses. Legislators were always mindful of having a good record of accomplishments on senior citizens' issues to brag about since seniors made up such a large bloc of those who actually voted, well over twenty percent.

The doctors kept up their advertising campaign that included a late March ad on the Op-Ed page in the *New York Times*. Rose Kryzak had seen this all before and she sent a letter to the editor:

"I am a senior citizen, 90 years old and remember that the medical profession warned us against Medicare. They told us it was socialized medicine and that we should not allow it to be enacted because doctors would leave their practice. It was as untrue and unethical then as it is today for the New York State Medical Society to threaten that there will be a reduction in access to health care and that doctors will shift their overcharges to the bills of their younger patients and blame it on their older patients."

Furious negotiations on the Medicare assignment bill heated up late in the session in June and early July. The State Medical Society still wanted to kill the bill. StateWide and other senior groups had created major pressure to pass the bill and both houses began drafting language. The bill was watered down but it passed. It set an incentive for doctors to reduce the number of overcharges. If ninety percent of doctor visits were billed at the assigned rate, then they would still be able to collect up to the fifteen percent overcharge allowable by Medicare. If less than ninety percent did so the amount of allowable overcharges would be limited, going down to five percent. The Medical Society sued and lost. The law went into effect though the State Department of Health made no serious effort to enforce it.

Legislators responded on two other major issues of concern for seniors. They passed the landmark Health Care Proxy law which allowed relatives or friends to sign a legal proxy to act for an incapacitated patient and they passed major changes to EPIC.

EPIC had still been plagued by complaints about the cost to participate and the confusing rules which included five different co-payments for drugs purchased. EPIC had not busted the state budget, it wasn't even enticing to many seniors. There were premiums to be paid quarterly to join the program or participants could choose to join via a deductible plan to just make co-payments once they had met the deductibles. Far from the hundreds of thousands expected to join, only 80,000 were in the program in mid-1990. 25,000 had left the program, some from death, but many simply didn't renew their membership.

Rose and StateWide began a push in late 1989 and throughout 1990 to simplify EPIC. A coalition of senior groups said the program was preventing many seniors from participating because it was "too complex, too confusing and too restrictive." As he prepared to run for re-election Governor Cuomo proposed changes in the program as well. The Medicare assignment campaign was a more high profile and controversial effort, but EPIC reform had popular support from legislators who had experience with the program, responding to concerns communicated to their offices about its complexity.

In July, as the Legislature was getting ready to end its session, improvements in EPIC were passed that would reduce the fees seniors paid and simplify the program, reducing the number of co-payments and capping out of pocket costs. It was another great victory. The "foot in the door" approach had worked.

The victory soon vanished though. The changes were to take effect on January 1, 1991 but they never did. The Persian Gulf Crisis erupted just a month later in August 1990, sending oil prices skyrocketing and pushing the United States into the beginning of a deep recession. After the November election in 1990, Governor Cuomo's budget office reported the state had a huge deficit. Cuomo proposed that all newly enacted spending including the EPIC reform legislation and tax cuts be deferred for the coming year to ease the extent of budget cuts in existing programs. The Legislature went along.

Before proposing these deferrals though Cuomo won re-election against divided Republican and Conservative candidates. The Republican candidacy of wealthy Pierre Rinfret who was recruited because he could finance his own campaign turned into a joke as Rinfret shot from the hip and paid little heed to the necessities of being a statewide candidate. Rank and file Republicans were so disenchanted that the Conservative Party candidate Herbert London nearly outpolled him. With a recession beginning to grip the nation, Cuomo easily won but only with 54% of the voters supporting him versus his divided opposition.

Just a month before Cuomo's re-election, Rose Kryzak cele-brated her ninetieth birthday at StateWide's convention in Albany and Governor Cuomo attended the convention for the third time as governor to pay special tribute to Rose. Cuomo especially enjoyed the evening because he was coming to a celebration, not to deliver a major policy-related speech. There would be no hoops to jump through regarding issues. He proceeded to give a tribute that only he could that seemed to sum up what Rose was all about:

"I am here for one person and that's Rose Kryzak. I'm not going to tell any funny stories about Rose. She makes you pay for months. See how she's listening. See how her ear is cocked? See the look on her face? She's waiting for any wisecracks. She will get no wisecracks from Mario Cuomo. She will get only respect from me. I've tried a few times with a little teasing. Forget about it, she makes you pay for months.

There are no words that capture everything about Rose perfectly. She's more than that. She's unique in my experience. I've never met a person quite like her...

What is it about Rose? Well, we all know she is a tough fighter, that she has been an advocate not just causes for senior citizens now. She's given herself to all kinds of causes her adult life.

She always will until the point when she finally is summoned by St. Peter to make the case for some disenfranchised band of angels. When she gets to Heaven, St. Peter, he'll never see anything like he'll see when she gets to Heaven. Wait til she starts organiz-ing the angels. 'This you call a good life! Look at the cloud he put you on probably because you are a woman.' But from now until the moment she is finally summoned she is going to be advocating, she's going to keep fighting.

Here's what happens tonight. I come, in okay? I sit next to her and give a few kisses. 'Rose, you look wonderful. Tell me Rose what do you think about the federal budget?' She said, 'The federal budget, this is terrible. We're going to organize. I've got buses. I'm going down there. I'm going to talk. This is the worst thing ever.'

1981 - The White House Conference. Does everyone know the story of the White House Conference and Rose? Can I tell about the White House Conference? Rose goes to the White House Conference. What's the big deal? It's just the White House, President of the United States of America, the most important person in the world. He has a conference. She's there. She wants to speak. She is not allowed to speak. It's not her place to speak and nobody invited Rose to speak.

The president didn't invite her to speak, the president's people didn't. Nobody, no official invited her to speak. As a matter of fact, she wasn't invited to speak.

So, what did she do? She got up to speak. She got up and everybody rushed to stop her.

'You can't speak lady, whoever you are. We don't care where you come from. You can't speak.' 'Yes, I can speak.' She takes out of her bag a microphone she has smuggled in. She gets up and insists on speaking. They couldn't stop her. They were bigger than she was. They were stronger that she was. They had more authority than she had. They were right and she was wrong. They had the rules with them, they had the regulations with them, the tradition with them.

She was smarter than they were and she was indomitable. She knew how to embarrass them and she was prepared to do it. She will not be put down. So, they back away and Rose made her presentation. And, in that little vignette, that little anecdote, you have Rose Kryzak.

What is her power? Ego, no, it's not ego. It's something some of us pray for. Some of us go all through our lives and never have. It's a great blessing. She has the capacity to feel passionately about things. She has the added blessing of selecting important things. You know a lot of us go all through life without that gift. We never get roused to the point of feeling deeply enough in something to give everything to.

Imagine the kind of life that is, not having something to believe in deeply that she gives herself to. Her whole life is filled with things she believes in profoundly to the core of her soul. She does a service for all the people around her. All those bills get done because of Rose. The great things in history get done because of people like Rose Kryzak.

She's an instruction to us. She shames us, especially some of us who are younger and supposed to have advantages over her. She shames us. By showing how much harder she can work, how much more effectively she can work. And, she inspires us particularly because she reminds us of the one great truth: that you ought to believe in something bigger than yourself. Maybe she doesn't deliver that sermon or deliver it in homily form that to be truly good, to be fulfilled as a human being you ought to believe in something bigger than yourself: God, a community, a family or a cause but she demonstrates it every day of her life and creates a lot of good things. That's what it takes. Her whole life is filled with things. And in doing so, she does a good service.

Happy birthday which is actually in a couple weeks. To celebrate all the people of this great state - 18 million approximately honor, thank and respect Rose Kryzak for all she has done and perfectly embodies."

And, Rose responded,

"The governor tried to tell you that I do nothing but work. I have a lot of fun doing it and I am very rewarded and that's why I am 90 and happy and feeling good. I am telling you if you keep on working and enjoy what you're doing, you'll be 90 and more.

*I want to tell you more. I want just to say this before I thank the governor for all the nice things he said about me. You know I am committed because I know as the governor told you I came from poor beginnings and I **do** know what it is like to be very, very poor and now that I have a little more I just don't feel comfortable to enjoy it completely. I have compassion when I think of the SSI recipient who doesn't have enough or the other people living on incomes below the poverty level. You know, it just makes it harder to enjoy what you've got. So, try a little bit, if you've never been poor, try to understand and maybe you'll work a little harder.*

That's why our governor who tells us, and I do believe that he came from poor beginnings like I did, not that we're rich, he's caring and listens and when I say he hasn't done enough yet he doesn't get angry and I hope he'll try to do better!

Thank you all for making my ninetieth birthday a happy one."

Rose continued to be honored on her 90th birthday. Newsday did a feature story on her in its Queens section and she gave the reporter quite a dose of her wit and logic: "I'm not going to sit down and retire. I'll continue doing what I'm doing. I don't have any great hobbies or talents. I can't sing or dance and I can't draw. But I can talk."

In the midst of the battle for Medicare assignment she couldn't resist taking a shot at doctors, "Money, that's the thing doctors don't want to give up. You notice doctors don't go to areas where they need doctors. The way they flock to Great Neck, you'd think there was an epidemic in Great Neck."

To note her 90th birthday, Rose and her family decided to establish an endowment fund for StateWide, which became the Rose Kryzak Legacy Fund. Rose and her family members gave over $3,000 to start the fund.

Rose maintained her concern not just about aging issues but national and world concerns at that momentous time. In the spring of 1990, just months after the Berlin Wall had come down, she wanted to comment on the debate about the "peace dividend," the military money that would be saved by ending the Cold War. She wrote on the front page of StateWide's newspaper, *Senior Action:*

"We need to rethink our concept of national security. The Soviet Union and the United States are cutting their military budgets. These savings must be used for human security. Money should be allocated for education so that every child can read. There should be more money for fighting drug disease so that every addict who wants to get help can get into a rehabilitation program. And, every American can get adequate and affordable health care. In addition, the peacetime budget can be used to build federally funded low and middle income housing. Tell your Congressman that a population that is well taken care of is the greatest national security."

Older New Yorkers for Dinkins

David Dinkins for Mayor

He has a consistent record of support for issues of particular concern to senior citizens.

Rose Kryzak on Dinkins campaign brochure for senior citizens, 1989

Governor Cuomo with Rose Kryzak at StateWide convention
to celebrate her 90th birthday, October 1990, Jane Gould and
Paul Harenberg are also at the table

Statewide members protesting outside Business Council offices against the Council's proposals to consolidate the State Office for the Aging and cut human services, early 1990's

Governor Cuomo, Rose Kryzak, and Assemblyman Paul Harenberg
share a laugh at an event in Queens

Michael and Anne Widzowski of Cohoes receiving a 1994 Senior
Citizen of Distinction Award from Governor Cuomo and Jane Gould,
Director of the New York State Office for the Aging

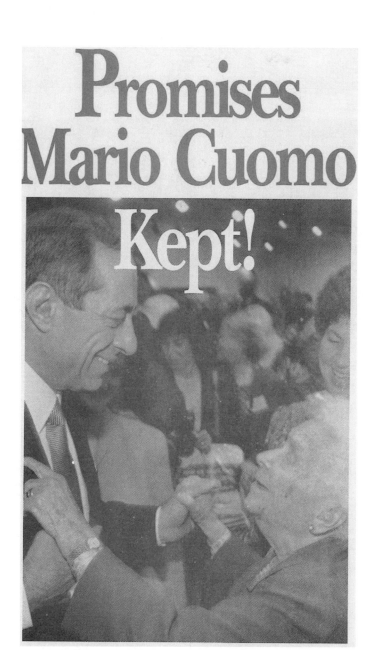

Cover of Cuomo campaign brochure for senior citizens, 1994

Rose Kryzak with long-time StateWide member Sister Bernadette Devlin of Catholic Charities in Brooklyn at one of Rose's last StateWide conventions in the late 1990's

StateWide Board President Mike Bishansky of Rockland County at an Albany press conference, voicing support for the Marchi-Lafayette bill to regulate prescription drug prices in New York; left to right Senator Nancy Larraine Hoffman, Senator Thomas Morahan, Senator John Marchi, Mike Bishansky, Assemblyman Ivan Lafayette, Shirley Ehrickhman of JPAC seniors, March 2000

Seniors from Binghamton area with their placards at the State Capitol in Albany as they board the StateWide-Citizen Action-Public Citizen bus to Montreal to buy prescription drugs, June 5, 2000

Hillary Clinton speaking at StateWide's 2000 annual convention,
October 30, 2000, as she was campaigning for the US Senate.
Daughter Chelsea joined her and is seated at head table

New York State Attorney General Eliot Spitzer addressing
StateWide convention, November 1, 2000 with Margaret Cuthbert,
Robert Miller, Michael Burgess at head table

Michael Burgess, StateWide President Bob Miller, Lani Sanjek and
Greg Olsen at StateWide convention, October 2000

President Clinton greeting Michael Burgess and his wife, Kate, at the White House, December 21, 2000. Mrs. Clinton invited them to one of the White House Christmas parties after she spoke at StateWide's convention

StateWide Board member Pearl Reeves of Queens speaking against the privatization of Social Security at a rally at the World Trade Center in Manhattan, June 2001, three months before it collapsed

Members of StateWide and the Rose Kryzak Action Alliance rally in
Philadelphia against the privatization of Social Security, 2001

"Granny D," Doris Haddock of New Hampshire who walked
across America at age 90 for campaign finance reform with
StateWide Board member and General Electric retiree activist
Helen Quirini at StateWide's 2001 convention

CHAPTER ELEVEN

RECESSION, DEFICITS, BUDGET CUTS

T HE RECESSION AND DEFICITS IN THE STATE BUDGET CONTINUED into 1991 and Governor Cuomo proposed major budget cuts including some in senior services. In February 1991, state labor unions, which had long been supportive of Cuomo held a huge rally with thousands of supporters outside the Governor's Mansion to oppose Cuomo's plans to eliminate thousands of state jobs. Senior advocacy organizations were on the defensive trying to restore funding rather than expand it. This defensive posture was to dominate advocacy efforts for most of the 1990's until a resurgent and soaring economy produced huge surpluses in Albany and later in Washington. The EPIC program changes were deferred for another year. In fact, the Legislature simply included language every year to defer the changes until 2000 when the program was greatly expanded. Budget deficits and tax increases would continue in the next three legislative sessions during the end of Cuomo's third term. Conservative and anti-tax groups attacked Cuomo and the legislative leaders and began funding a new organization, CHANGE-NY, to fight state fiscal policies and challenge incumbent legislators, especially Republicans who voted for tax increases.

A coalition of human services groups pushed hard for increased taxes on the wealthy to balance the budget rather than cuts in human services. The kisses and sweet words on Rose's ninetieth birthday between her and Governor Cuomo didn't last long. Rose was such a determined advocate and principled believer that she never let the birthday lovefest cloud her vision. She was terribly disappointed with Cuomo's policies. She continued to send him letters, but her April 16, 1991 letter to him got quite pointed,

"For the first time since you became Governor, I feel so alienated from your present political philosophy. Your determination to demand that working people and the middle class people carry an unfair share of taxes...puts us at opposite ends of the human pole.

It is hard for me to understand how you can think that the working people and the middle class people can continue to bear the burden year after year of the budget cuts. Why should not the rich and big corporations make up more of the burden by paying a fair share of taxes?

Governor Cuomo, you are a very intelligent man. I know you could play a national leadership role — in the health care crisis for a good health care program and a progressive tax system for all Americans. What is stopping you?"

She didn't like his response, which included some standard rhetoric about the need to not raise taxes to keep the state competitive so that it would have the future revenues to afford more social spending. Sending me copies of the correspondence, she jotted a note to me, " The enclosed are the letters that I sent the governor and his response. I thought his response was long and empty."

Cuomo's budget problems in Albany were the backdrop for a greater national drama for him as 1991 drew to a close. After passing up an opportunity to run for president in 1988, Cuomo flirted so much with it that the media had dubbed him "Hamlet on the Hudson." In the fall of 1991 though, Cuomo publicly acknowledged what he never had before: that he was seriously considering running for president. It was hard for him to resist since all polls of Democrats showed him as favorite for the Democratic nomination. The media was full of stories about his potential entry into the Democratic primary in New Hampshire. He said though that his first responsibility was to the State of New York and he wouldn't run if he couldn't resolve the state's fiscal crisis. Many felt he was allowing Republican State Senate Majority Leader Ralph Marino to have veto power over his presidential aspirations.

The national media descended on Albany in December for the last filing day to enter the New Hampshire primary. An airplane waited at Albany airport to take Cuomo to New Hampshire. Finally, he announced that he would not run because of the budget problems. Others speculated he didn't really want to or that there were other reasons. Democrats were let down. They were convinced that not only would he have beaten ex-Massachusetts Senator Paul Tsongas who won the New Hampshire primary but that he would have knocked out Arkansas Governor Bill Clinton who eventually won the nomination. And, though it didn't appear so easy in late 1991, many felt in hindsight that if Clinton could beat Bush, Cuomo would have crushed Bush and been elected president since he didn't have the baggage of Clinton's extramarital affairs and questions about his truthfulness on other personal matters.

While Cuomo wouldn't go to New Hampshire, Rose was off to Cuba. Despite her role in mainstream politics in New York, she remained sympathetic to Communism and the visit was a part of that. She expressed admiration for what the socialist country was trying to do, but she was appalled at some of the primitive conditions. The Communist Party's *People's Daily* newspaper wrote about her trip as she talked about how she was confident "they would make it" because of the spirit of the Cuban people.

Rose kept active into her 90's and she continued to take the bus to Albany to meet with legislators and speak for other causes as well. In 1992, she got involved in supermarket pricing. Consumer advocates were pushing to pass legislation to require item pricing in grocery stores so that each item was individually marked rather than have a large sign by a group of similar merchandise. Electronic scanners were being introduced in supermarkets and grocery store owners said that accuracy would be even greater. Once again it was Rose who clearly told the press in practical terms what it meant for seniors like her if they had to look at the unit price underneath a group of cans on the bottom shelf, "If I have to bend down to check what the price is for a can of tuna fish, I might never get up again." That quote and her picture were prominent in the Albany newspaper the next day.

In July of 1992, Rose spent another week with my family in the North Country. Bill Clinton had just been nominated for president at the Democratic National Convention and Rose stayed riveted to CNN to watch the post-convention news and analysis. On the trip, she joined us with my extended family at my aunt and uncle's home on the St. Lawrence River. She loved the beauty and the serenity of the river. She hated to leave but she had to get back to work, so at age 92 she flew alone out of tiny Massena airport in a small commuter plane.

The budget crisis in New York State had taken its toll and threatened StateWide in 1991 when money for its patient's rights hotline was eliminated from the budget. Bonnie Ray saw her staff eliminated and her own job threatened. She kept the organization going through 1992 but it was a tremendous burden on her to continue StateWide's function with little or no help at times until the middle of 1993 when funding was restored. The organization was fortunate to have such committed members though. Ruth

Hawes of Sullivan County was a very knowledgeable, dedicated, organized senior who served as President in the early 1990's. She was followed by Mike Widzowski, a passionate advocate from Cohoes who studied the issues, felt strongly about them and often testified for StateWide in Albany. Rose Kryzak continued to serve on the Board as a President Emeritus and she continued her advocacy.

Despite the funding crisis, StateWide also was successful in getting a major bill passed regulating the deposit of pre-need funeral funds. Funeral homes fought the bill, but consumer protection was needed since there were few laws governing what would happen to funds deposited in advance to a funeral home if the business was sold or went bankrupt.

Rose also stayed active in New York City politics and local community activities. She worked very closely in Queens with members of the State Assembly from her area, especially her own representative, Catherine Nolan. She also enjoyed working with other members from Queens including Audrey Pheffer, Denis Butler, Alan Hevesi, Tom Catapano, Nettie Mayersohn and later Mark Weprin and Brian McLaughlin. She liked working with Helene Weinstein, Frank Barbaro and Rhoda Jacobs from Brooklyn and of course, worked with Jim Tallon and Richard Gottfried as Chairs of the Health Committee. She had a long relationship with Jim Brennan of Brooklyn who worked with her in the community on public power and energy issues in the 1970's. Of course, she was closest with Paul Harenberg who remained as Chair of the Aging Committee until 1997. She had many other admirers in both parties in the Legislature.

She also loved working with her local senior and community agencies like the Queens Interagency Council on Aging (QUICA). She was active for many years in QUICA and was an officer. She would make trips to Albany on their behalf too. Dr. Linda Leest, head of the Council recounted how one time in the mid-1990s she joined Rose for a trip to Albany and they came back on Amtrak in one of the worst snowstorms in years to hit the east coast. There was no food left on the train. Rose was hungry and exhausted but she still was making other people feel good. "Rose was a real trooper. "We cut (the remaining food) into tiny pieces," Linda said. Finally, they got back to New York at midnight. Mayor Giuliani closed the city and Rose had no way to get her back to Queens. She called her granddaughter, Jeannie, and they got permission from NYPD to let her be picked up. Jeannie got there at 1:30 in the morning to take her home.

She also worked for the re-election of Mayor David Dinkins in a rematch with Republican Rudy Giuliani in 1993. It was another close election but this time, city voters who were reflecting the anxiety of the times, defeated Dinkins and ushered in the Giuliani era. Rose was getting frailer and wondering how much longer she would be able to go to Albany alone on the bus to take part in advocacy efforts. She was also feeling dispirited as 1993 came to a close. Her 79-year-old sister, the youngest in her family, had died. While going through some of her sister's belongings, Rose found some papers that indicated that she was not born on October 15, 1900 as she had always believed, but a year earlier on the same date in 1899. Many older people were often uncertain about their ages because records from their childhood were often not available. Rose had to adjust her age and tell everyone she was really 94, not 93.

Universal Health Care

In the early 1990's, universal health care became the main battle cry of seniors and a coalition of over 70 organizations in the state concerned about health care. For seniors like Rose Kryzak, national health care was an unfulfilled promise and every year she and others would raise the issue as the only real solution to the myriad of problems discussed about the lack of or inadequacy of coverage for health care. About 40 million Americans didn't have health care coverage and advocates kept noting that the United States and South Africa were the only two industrialized countries without such a system.

There was a sense among many health care advocates that a single-payer national health care system would be enacted in the 1990's. The country's attention had turned to domestic issues after the end of the Cold War. Arthur Flemming, the former Secretary of Health, Education and Welfare and Wilbur Cohen, one of the architects of Medicare, toured the country, including Albany, to push the idea. They even predicted it would happen in a few short years. They seemed to have been right when Bill Clinton was elected president. At the end of his first year in office in 1993, he addressed Congress and held up a "Health Security card" that he said he wanted every American to have. He appointed his wife to spearhead the administration's efforts. The complicated hybrid approach that included government and private insurance went down in flames with the famous Harry and Louise ads run by the threatened insurance industry.

At the state level, Democrats had also tried to get a statewide system established. Like so many other initiatives at that time, New York health care activists took their cues again from the neighboring state of Massachusetts which, under the leadership of Governor Michael Dukakis, had passed a universal health care bill.

In 1991, Assemblyman Richard Gottfried, Chair of the Health Care, introduced a comprehensive bill, NY Health, to enact a state single payer universal health care system. This was the kind of bill that Rose and others who had struggled for social insurance really wanted and they supported it with enthusiasm. StateWide made the bill its top priority in 1992. The bill passed the Assembly in May 1992 but there was no Senate sponsor of the bill. Republicans in the Senate were much more sympathetic to the views of doctors, health providers and insurers and they felt that the Gottfried bill was socialized medicine. Even if they couldn't pass universal health care, advocates were determined to expand coverage, especially for children.

Bonnie Ray decided it was time to link up the advocacy power of seniors and Statewide to help children's groups. In fact, by the end of the 1980's, annual cost of living adjustments in Social Security had been successful in dramatically cutting the elderly poverty rate. The recession in the early 1990's though would drive more and more children into poverty. In 1993, Bonnie teamed with Ellie Ward of Statewide Youth Advocacy on a joint intergenerational campaign, Our Voices United, and StateWide members helped push the passage of Child Health Plus which provided health coverage for children up to age 12. At its annual convention StateWide selected several priorities that would benefit both seniors and children. Seniors came to the Capitol to push for the program. Some legislators wondered why they were so forceful in their support, but StateWide's members believed everyone should have health care especially their grandchildren's generation..

Generational Unity

Like any grandmother, Rose's concern for children was genuine, not just rhetorical. In December of 1990, she had one of her most joyful experiences as an advocate. She went to PS 69 in Jackson Heights, Queens to speak to the fourth grade class about her work and the origins of Social Security. Many of the kids had never seen anybody 90 years old! After she left, the teacher asked the students to send thank you letters to Rose. She made quite an impact on the class.

Dear "Aunt" Rose:

We were very pleased to meet you. Your presentation was great I liked when you told us that Franklin Delano Roosevelt helped put people who were homeless into a camp. I also liked when you told us that health care is a problem for all people whether you're young or old. It costs too much money.

We will help old people cross the streets and carry their bags for them.

It was a pleasure that you came and talked to us.

> *Your friend,*
> *Abhishek*

Dear "Aunt"Rose:

Thank you for coming and talking to us about elderly people. It's sad to know that elderly people aren't getting proper health care. It's wrong for people of all ages to have to pay so much to go to a doctor. I hope that by the time I retire I won't have to pay so much.

Franklin Delano Roosevelt must have been very smart to be able to divide money in such a way that there was enough money to pay other countries. Also he took homeless people, gave them food and a place to sleep. Then training them for a job. I wish somebody would do that today to help the homeless.

I learned that we could help old people by helping them cross the street or giving them a seat on the bus or subway. I learned a lot today.

> *Your friend,*
> *Sarah*

Mrs. Kryzak:

Thank you for your wonderful presentation and taking your time and spending it talking to us. I found it interesting that Franklin Delano Roosevelt set up a WPA law for homeless people. Without him, their lives would have been worthless. They would have gone to shelters and people said here's bread and a bed then you feel plain useless.

In the Gulf crisis you're Dear right. No one should lose an ounce of blood over prices of oil.

People do need cheap health care. It is important to enjoy living and not spending hundreds of dollars on health care.

> *Thank you for coming.*
> *Your friend,*
> *Brendan*

She loved the letters she received and wanted them published in StateWide's newspaper

Young people were also asking Rose to help them. After she spoke to students at Louis Armstrong Middle School in East Elmhurst in early 1992, the students must have realized she had some power. Rose got letters from some students like this one:

Our class is starting a petition against Joe Camel cigarettes, RJ Reynolds and RJR Nabisco. We are starting a petition because Joe Camel entices children to smoke but we don't want that.

Mrs. Norman is going to send to you a petition and we are asking you to get as many signatures as possible. We want to let RJ Reynolds and RJR Nabisco know we are boycotting their products until they stop using Joe Camel.

> *Sincerely,*
> *Natasha Kim*

Rose had made a impression on the children just as she had with her peers. The children sensed she was a committed and compassionate woman who cared about them.

CHAPTER TWELVE

TRANSITION: CHANGING NEW YORK

IN THE EARLY AND MID-1990'S THE FACES WHO HAD DOMINATED Albany for many years were quickly gone. In Albany, Speaker Miller was indicted and replaced as Assembly Speaker by Saul Weprin from Queens in 1993. Rose had known Weprin from her involvement in the borough and she liked him. She was excited about working with him after having little enthusiasm for Miller.

New York politics and its leaders who had seemed entrenched in their power experienced great upheaval in 1993 and 1994. The long-time State Comptroller, Ned Regan, resigned to take another position. Soon, State Attorney General Robert Abrams who had been defeated in a run for US Senate against Senator Alfonse D'Amato announced he was leaving. The State Legislature meeting as one body with Democrats having more total members elected Carl McCall, Cuomo's designated running mate in 1982 and a former State Senator and United Nations officials as the new Comptroller. For Attorney General, they elected Assemblyman Oliver Koppell who had been the sponsor of the Home Energy Fair Practice Act, the "utility bill of rights." Then, early in 1994, the new Speaker Weprin, died of cancer. Democrats elected Sheldon Silver of Manhattan to replace him.

And, late in 1993, it seemed possible Cuomo might retire, but he loved the job and decided to run again. He viewed the 1994 race as a challenge, whether he could withstand the Republican tide, which seemed to be sweeping the country. After twelve years as governor, many New Yorkers had grown tired of Cuomo though and wanted a change. Many were even angry with him, viewing him as a "tax and spend" symbol of what was wrong with the state, especially as it was struggling to pull out of the recession. A man who had been so popular in 1986 that he had won by the largest margin in state history now was in danger of losing.

What's a Pataki?

Running against Cuomo was George Pataki, a previously little known but ambitious state senator who was a favorite of US Senator Alfonse D'Amato, the kingpin of state Republican politics. Republican leaders wanted to find an ethnic Catholic who favored abortion rights and the death penalty and preferably came from the New York City suburbs. Pataki fit the bill even though other Republicans sought the nomination. When D'Amato and state Republican Party Chairman Bill Powers decided Pataki was their man, they used their influence to push Pataki and quash the chances of other contenders.

As Peter Slocum wrote in his book, *From Rocky to Pataki,* put it,

"George Pataki's timing was perfect. The Republican Party was rebounding, finally, after years of statewide defeats that drained morale and money out of the once-proud party. The old Rockefeller moderate party had faded away and it took a long time to build anything back, partly because the primary source of money dried up."

Pataki had been a popular and affable local politician who had always been successful. He had been Mayor of Peekskill, a small northern Westchester County city, and then won a seat in the State Assembly. He had also previously worked for State Senator Mary Goodhue, a long-time office-holder in Westchester. Two years earlier though, Pataki, challenged Goodhue for her seat in a primary with the backing of CHANGE-NY, the insurgent group of conservative Republicans who viewed the incumbent Senate leadership as too accommodating to Cuomo and the Democrats in supporting tax hikes to balance the state's deficits. Pataki attacked his former mentor for being in Florida during budget votes in Albany and he eked out a 500-vote victory in the primary and became a State Senator by beating his Democratic opponent in November.

In running against Cuomo, Pataki touted the conservative line that New York State was overtaxed and that he would sign the death penalty. He and the Republican Party blamed everything bad in the state on Cuomo and hung the word "liberal" around his neck.

Cuomo and his administration had used the powers of his office to do everything possible to run for re-election. In October toward the end of the campaign, the governor held an event to honor seniors of distinction for the first time. Rose was one of those to be honored. The honorees were to simply express thanks and sit down. Not Rose though. When she came up, she told the governor and Jane Gould that she had something to say, more than just a thank you. She stole the show as she asked, "What's a Pataki?" She said she had been to Albany many times and had "never seen a Pataki, but now D'Amato said he has found one." The place exploded with laughter and so did Cuomo. Once again, Rose Kryzak with her simple logic had reduced the campaign to its simplest terms and made Cuomo's case for him. There was no wonder every Democrat wanted Rose on their brochures that went to seniors. The Cuomo campaign printed special outreach materials for older voters and displayed a picture of Rose talking with Cuomo. Rose's sense of comedy was also ratified when David Letterman did a skit on his show called "What's a Pataki?"

Pataki won the Republican primary and led in the polls throughout the early fall and into October. Democrats were nervous but hoped that Cuomo could pull out the victory. In mid-October, President Clinton flew into Albany to campaign for him. The tide seemed to finally turn two weeks before the election when Republican New York City Mayor Rudolph Giuliani endorsed Cuomo. Republicans were outraged and called him a "Judas." Cuomo surged in the polls with this endorsement by the popular mayor of the other party, and wiped out Pataki's lead in a tracking poll and even opened up a sizable lead of his own for a few days.

Giuliani's endorsement was a week too soon though and the tracking poll reflected only a momentary surge of media exposure rather than a change in the underlying mood of the electorate. By the end of the second week after the endorsement as Election Day approached, a backlash occurred. Republicans exploited the fact that the Mayor of New York City wanted Cuomo and that was bad for upstate. Pataki crushed Cuomo in upstate New York and won the election by 49% - 45%, ending two decades of Democratic control of the Governor's Mansion in the post-Rockefeller era. Karen Burstein the Democratic candidate for Attorney General who had defeated the appointed incumbent Oliver Koppell in the primary, was also defeated by Republican Dennis Vacco.

StateWide was in transition again too. Just as all the political changes swept Albany and Washington, I wanted to get back into senior advocacy and in late 1994, the AARP was interviewing for positions for a new Albany office they had opened. I was a finalist but did not get the job. I was disappointed because I knew I had the experience for the job. Within days, irony intervened and a better opportunity appeared. I was going to be headed back into senior advocacy, in my old job!

Bonnie Ray told me she was planning to leave StateWide the following year and was concerned about finding someone able to take over the organization and keep it going in an effective fashion. She loved the job but it had been difficult with funding problems and she also wanted to be near to her mother and family in Vermont. She asked me if I was interested in returning and, of course, I was. So, just as funding for my job at the Non-Profit Resource Center was becoming less certain, I looked forward to going back to StateWide. I told Rose and she was pleased that the organization wouldn't suffer when Bonnie left. After eight years as director, Bonnie had earned the affection and respect of many in the advocacy and government circles in Albany and StateWide gave her a going away party. I returned to StateWide as Director on July 1, 1995.

It was quickly clear that this was going to be unlike my first tenure at StateWide. Though I knew Rose and many of the seniors who were still active, the issues of the day were different and so was the organization. There was much to do to re-build an active network of seniors. I was lucky to have Greg Olsen and Iliana Schreiber in the office in Albany while Lani Sanjek was still with us working in New York City. In western New York, Bea Berman was our field representative and her husband, Max, was board president. Max was a union activist with the UAW retirees and together, they had extensive contacts in the greater Buffalo area. Bea would organize seniors to visit their Congressman and she often appeared on a local cable television program.

There were also strong groups in the North Country and in

Rockland County where seniors were very active in health care issues. In the North Country, the state's least populated area, StateWide had a long favorable reputation and when Robert Miller took over as the regional leader he built it up again, recruiting over 20 local senior clubs to join. New leadership also came from the Rockland County Community College senior club and one of its leaders, Mike Bishansky. Both he and Bob Miller would go on to become board presidents of StateWide in the ensuing years. The Cayuga County Council of Senior Citizens provided a base for leadership activities in central New York with the assistance and enthusiasm of Nelsa Selover, the Director of the county Office for the Aging. Fortunately, the organization's finances were in much better shape than in the 1980's.

The Congressional elections of 1994 which made Newt Gingrich of Georgia the House Speaker were as dispiriting for those in the human services community as the election of Ronald Reagan had been fourteen years earlier. For the first time in forty years, the Republican Party had taken control of Congress. The Republican sweep was complete across the nation. Not a single incumbent Republican lawmaker lost as Newt Gingrich led his party to a 52-seat pickup and control of the House of Representatives for the first time in forty years. Republicans also swept to control of the US Senate with Bob Dole as Majority Leader. In a letter to the editor in Senior Action, Mary Gale, one of StateWide's original activists from New York City reflected the political and personal attitude of many of StateWide's members:

"Today is a sad day in our lives because we had a national election where many of the winners supported the "Contract with America," which in my opinion, goes in the direction of denying help and assistance to America's neediest, our children and grand-

children. I suppose one of the reasons I have lived to be 94 years old is because I insist on seeing a better world, a world of Peace and Friendship. And also I hate to leave my beautiful friends who are working so hard to bring about such a world. I want to stay around long enough to help the New World celebrate. So - be well and keep going and doing!"

My job changed in another important way. With the Republican takeover of Congress and Pataki's victory in Albany, the entire focus of senior advocacy changed. Since the beginning of the senior movement, advocates had always pushed for more funding for services at the state and federal level and the improvement of Medicare. In 1995 though, advocacy efforts were entirely defensive, trying to stop the threat of budget cuts in Medicare in Washington as well as cuts in Medicaid. In Albany the battle was to stop cuts in Medicaid as well as other cuts in state services.

Seniors and advocates were nervous because they knew that Gingrich and Pataki had come to power with clear plans to cut taxes and roll back social and health programs. In Albany, it was a winter of discontent. Though Pataki faced a $5 billion deficit he pushed for a massive multi-year cut in income taxes coupled with major cuts in Medicaid and other services. With a battle mentality, Pataki and his allies said they were prepared to close state government and send workers home if the state budget was not enacted by April 1, the start of the new fiscal year. Scared Democrats who controlled the Assembly had already announced their own tax cut proposal. Republican State Party chief Bill Powers said he was raising money for ads attacking Assembly Democrats in their districts and he predicted Republicans would take over that chamber in 1996.

State workers unions rebelled at the talk of closing state government. Many lived in the Saratoga and Rennselaer counties in the district of the new Majority Leader Joseph Bruno who was going along with Pataki. Bruno who was close to State Republican Party Chair Bill Powers, had ascended to power following a post-election November coup that toppled Ralph Marino of Long Island. Marino had not been early or eager to support Pataki, a freshman member of Marino's Senate majority. The union outrage was being vented against Bruno and he began to feel politically threatened for the first time in his career. A massive demonstration was held in which close to 10,000 persons came to the Capitol grounds to protest Pataki's budget. Most of the protesters were African-Americans and Hispanics bussed in by unions in New York City. Pataki ordered hundreds of state troopers to handle the demonstrations. He also ordered new security measures at the State Capitol, closing to the public the Hall of Governors on the Second Floor outside his office, the same hall where Rose Kryzak had led the final rally for EPIC eight years earlier. The media dubbed the State Capitol, " Fort Pataki."

Advocates for the homeless and human services set up a shantytown of cardboard boxes called "Camp Patakiville" behind the State Capitol and a few legislators joined them as they slept overnight in the winter cold of Albany.

For seniors, Pataki's worst damage was the threat to the Medicaid program which he targeted for substantial cuts. Two thirds of the Medicaid budget was spent on long-term care. So there was no easy way to cut it without affecting seniors. Pataki took aim at the personal care program, which provided non-medical home care services. He also proposed eliminating the federal government's annual cost of living adjustment for SSI recipients using it instead to lower the state's $86 monthly supplement to the program for most beneficiaries. This proposal would directly take money from the state's poorest citizens while tax cuts were going to all including the wealthy.

Even though Rose didn't know or support the new Governor, she always wanted to get to personally know those in office, because she felt she would be able to develop a relationship. She never got in to see Pataki though she tried during one trip to Albany after he took office. She was so offended feeling like she was treated" like a speck of dust," as Linda Leest of QUICA recalled. "They closed the door right in her face."

While the budget battle was unfolding, another White House Conference on the Aging was approaching. It should have been held every ten years. It was still the prerogative of the president to hold the event and President Bush did not commit to hold the conference in 1991. Only after President Clinton took office were plans made to have another conference in 1995. Once again, Rose Kryzak would go with the New York delegation for what was a very lackluster event compared to the 1981 conference.

In March, Rose Kryzak and 450 seniors and advocates were gathering in Saratoga Springs for a state conference to precede the White House Conference on Aging scheduled for May. After twenty years at the State Office for the Aging, Jane Gould left as Republicans took control. Maribeth Bersani who had worked as Executive Deputy Director in the agency served as Acting Director, overseeing preparations for the new White House Conference. The state conference was to discuss issues and develop priorities of the delegates and other seniors from New York.

Rose and a band of 150 activists decided that since they were in Saratoga they would march down Broadway to Senator Bruno's downtown district office there to complain about the proposed $1.2 billion in Medicaid cuts that eliminated housekeeping services, home health programs and adult day care. Governor Pataki had just succeeded in passing and signing the death penalty in New York and some charged that Pataki was extending it to the elderly with a moratorium on nursing home beds, limits on personal care and quicker hospital discharges of Medicaid patients. They donned red shirts with a slash through a circle that said "Medicaid Cuts." The back of the shirts said, "Not on the backs of seniors." The media covered the visit as Rose, at age 95, and others led the delegation into the office and met with the receptionist.

Rose was thrilled with the media coverage and felt she had made an impact. StateWide put out a press release saying that this 95-year-old woman was so upset about Pataki's budget that she was prepared to come to Albany every week to fight it. Despite Rose's exhilaration, the trips to Albany almost killed her. She was so tired when she returned to Queens that she went to bed and couldn't take any calls the next day. She also had fallen out of bed and needed help. Still, by May she was back in Washington for the White House Conference on Aging. Bonnie Ray who was also a delegate to the White House Conference found it a waste of time. The dynamic energy of the previous three conferences was gone. Perhaps it was because the Gingrich era had just begun and seemed to limit expansions of human services.

Eventually, Pataki and Bruno backed off their plans to close state government. Then, after a long struggle over the budget which wasn't passed until June, Pataki got his multi-year tax cut but many of his cuts in Medicaid were rejected. Pataki did welcome seniors to the Governor's Mansion on Senior Citizens Day in May. It was the last time he ever attended the official event. In the coming years, he sent Lieutenant Governor Mary Donahue or Bernadette Castro, the Parks Commisioner. His mother always attended as a hostess though.

Pataki did campaign in senior centers when he ran for re-election. Unlike Cuomo though, Pataki would never meet himself with major senior citizens' groups and he turned down every invitation by StateWide and even the AARP to address large gatherings. He felt no need to show he was interested or committed to older New Yorkers once he passed his property tax relief program, STAR in his first term and passed the death penalty.

StateWide did develop very strong relationships with Republican leaders in the next few years. StateWide worked closely with the new Attorney General, Dennis Vacco, as he aggressively took on HMOs for denying care for their plan members. Vacco invited StateWide to serve on a new senior citizens advisory panel he created in the office and he also awarded StateWide $20,000 from fines assessed on HMOs to run a managed care education project. Over the years, StateWide always had a strong relationship with the Attorney General's office because of that office's role in protecting consumers. In the 1980's Attorney General Robert Abrams attended StateWide conventions and after he defeated Vacco in 1998, Eliot Spitzer and StateWide worked closely on lawsuits against drug companies and other consumer issues.

In the late 1990's the role of HMOs become the central health care issue for StateWide and other health care and consumer advocacy organizations. The HMOs were aggressively marketing to seniors in Medicare as well as becoming dominant in the private insurance market. As they attempted to greatly restrain costs though, they became targets of consumer advocates and politicians who accused them of ordering "drive by deliveries" for mothers to give birth as outpatients and "drive by mastectomies" for breast cancer patients. They were also attacked for denying life saving care for terminally ill patients and they were accused of giving pay incentives to doctors to deny care as well as "gag" orders to prevent doctors from talking about more expensive additional care options.

Also jumping on the HMO bandwagon in 1997 was Pataki's Lieutenant Governor Betsy McGaughey Ross who supposedly had been selected by Senator Alfonse D'Amato to be on the ticket to attract women. She was a political novice who was only known for a scathing critique of President Clinton's health care plan in the early 1990's. She soon proved that she would not be beholden to her Republican patrons and she became such an embarrassment to Pataki that he announced in 1997 that she wouldn't be on the ticket again. She ended up switching parties and ran unsuccessfully for the Democratic nomination to oppose Pataki.

Unwittingly, StateWide got dragged into this political hornet's nest in the spring of 1997 when the Lieutenant Governor who had been working with StateWide on HMO issues accepted an invitation to attend the Seniorama, a large event for hundreds of North Country seniors at the Lake Placid Olympic Arena. That was before Governor Pataki dumped her from his ticket and began treating her as a pariah.

To the Governor's office she was not irrelevant though. They feared she was running against Alfonse D'Amato. They wanted to make her life as miserable as possible. So, the day before the Lake Placid event, the word went out from the Chairman of the Essex County Board of Supervisors. He was dis-inviting the Lieutenant Governor. Someone in Albany seemed to have forced him or else Senator Stafford did.

The Lieutenant Governor decided not to attend though. She sent five staff people including the high powered Thomas Spargo, an election law attorney. They came with hundreds of flyers that said, *"Who Kept Betsy Away?"* The local county officials didn't want them around and took the box and threw it in the trash.

CHAPTER THIRTEEN

WITHERING ON THE VINE: FIGHTING THE GINGRICH REVOLUTION

WHILE SENIORS WERE BATTLING TO MAINTAIN STATE FUNDING a bigger battle was brewing in Washington. House Speaker Newt Gingrich proposed a $270 billion cut in Medicare, mostly in reductions to hospitals, nursing homes and home care providers. There was also a serious effort to turn Medicaid into a state block grant program which was turned back. While Social Security's finances were more of a long-term problem, Medicare was projected to go broke much sooner than Social Security and it had already been targeted for budget cuts. Republicans were also proposing major changes in the program that would make it more market-oriented.

Gingrich's Medicare plan was proposed late in the summer and only one hearing was held. Gingrich was viewed by seniors and their advocates as playing a cute game of saying he was "saving Medicare" as he proposed to decimate it. It was accurate that his proposal was only to cut the rate of growth of Medicare not cut the actual amount of dollars from year to year. However, health care costs had been rising quickly in the 1990's and his proposals for slower growth were viewed as leading to major cuts.

Gingrich really wanted to privatize it in some fashion by developing more attractive private plans, such as HMOs, that would offer more services than traditional Medicare. Gingrich loved to talk a lot and explain his game plans. He indicated that he didn't want to abolish Medicare outright because that would be unpopular and politically foolish. Instead, his plan would force the traditional program to compete against better alternative plans and the traditional Medicare program would "wither on the vine" because, in a few years, a sizable minority of seniors would have left the traditional Medicare plan. It was that phrase which stuck in the minds of seniors and led them to fierce opposition of his proposals. Seniors from the National Council of Senior Citizens broke into the one public hearing wearing t-shirts and seeking to garner public attention to fight back this quick effort to radically change the program. In Albany, Helen Quirini attacked Gingrich, "I'm angry about what is happening in our country with the way the GOP, which stands for 'Get Older People' is out to destroy Medicare, one of the most successful covenants passed by our government over 30 years ago." That quote made the front page of the *Legislative Gazette*, the weekly newspaper at the Legislature.

At the end of the summer in 1995, we also celebrated the sixtieth anniversary of Social Security and the thirtieth birthday of Medicare that summer. StateWide joined with other groups to hold an event at the Delaware Avenue Senior Center in Albany that August to mark the occasion and to defend the program.

Gingrich and the Republican leadership meanwhile attempted to neutralize the power of the AARP by inviting them into early meetings about proposals to change the program. On the Senate side though, Senator Alan Simpson of Wyoming, a vocal opponent of the AARP, held hearings to look into the organization's business activities and question whether it deserved to maintain tax exempt status while it profited from some of its sales of insurance and other products. This intimidation of the organization at this critical time in debating Medicare's future didn't help seniors to fight back. Gingrich's efforts were thwarted though by President Clinton in a showdown that led to the infamous shutdown of the federal government.

Clinton vetoed the Medicare plan. Gingrich and the Republicans received most of the public blame and ridicule. In the end, Congress approved major cuts in the program but they were reduced to a little over $110 billion over five years. In 1999 and 2000, Congress realized it went too far as hospitals and other health care providers successfully forced them to restore some funding.

The final legislation did contain a number of major changes in Medicare that would make it more market-oriented. Some in Congress wanted to go further. Senator John Kyl of Arizona and Congressman Bill Archer of Texas proposed a bill to let doctors be in the Medicare program but also have private contracts with seniors where they could charge whatever they wanted. The law said they would have to opt out of Medicare for two years if they did this. In response to the Kyl-Archer bill, StateWide joined with other senior and health care advocates to establish an informal coalition, the New York Network for Action on Medicare (NYNAM). The coalition set out immediately to generate thousands of calls and letters to Congressional offices of New York representatives to oppose the Kyl-Archer bill and counter the effort and scare tactics of the Seniors Coalition, an organization that worked in tandem with the Republican Party and big business, especially the pharmaceutical industry. The Coalition's efforts persuaded one Congressman, Ben Gilman, to withdraw his support as a co-sponsor.

NYNAM continued to meet monthly in New York with other advocates connected by telephone from Albany and Binghamton. One of the provisions of the Balanced Budget Act of 1997 called for the appointment of a Bipartisan Commission on the Future of Medicare. NYNAM organized efforts along with groups in other states to promote the strengthening and protection of Medicare. The national coalition developed a position paper and platform and StateWide Assistant Director Lani Sanjek traveled to Washington to represent the national coalition at a press conference with Congressman Jim McDermott and Senator Paul Wellstone.

Social Security Again

In the late 1990's, the future of Social Security also took center stage in national issues. The Republican takeover of Congress and the high flying stock market emboldened conservative organizations to promote the privatization of Social Security. While some wanted to completely scrap the system in favor of a privatized pension system in which workers would invest in the markets, the more mainstream conservative position was to divert two percent of the payroll tax to investment in stock funds. To negate the influence of the powerful senior lobby, most proposals for change promised that current beneficiaries would not see any changes. While this approach sounded appealing to many Americans and polls showed support for it, the support dropped when persons were asked if they would accept lower guaranteed benefits. The lower benefits or an increase in the retirement age would be required because the Social Security Trust Fund would be losing the money diverted to private accounts for future generations.

New organizations like Economic Security 2000 popped up to develop grassroots support for privatization. Another organization, Americans Discuss Social Security, held a series of hearings about the issue around the country and President Clinton also participated in hearings co-sponsored by the AARP and other organizations. By 1998, these groups seemed to have convinced the media and had the momentum in Washington. It seemed to many seniors and their advocates that just as welfare had been overhauled, powerful forces now seemed to have the momentum to end "Social Security-as-we-know-it" and "Medicare-as-we-know-it."

The proposed privatization plans were not grassroots movements coming from older people but were being generated by conservative economic think tanks like the Cato Institute and other national groups. Like Gingrich, they were using a sophisticated propaganda campaign to sell their proposals not as privatization but as efforts to reform and "save" Social Security and Medicare. Marilyn Moon of the Urban Institute, perhaps the most thoughtful national defender of social insurance responded with an article entitled, "Can Social Security Survive its Saviors?"

It wasn't just conservative Republicans touting this proposal. New York's senior Senator Daniel Patrick Moynihan, considered to be the scholar and expert on social programs, unveiled a proposal with Senator Bob Kerrey of Nebraska that called for a reduction of the payroll tax by two percent with workers able to voluntarily use that money to establish a private account.

In 1999, the vacuum on the left ended when labor, minorities and church groups formed the Campaign for America's Future. The tide began to turn among Democrats in Congress and the president when they began to hear from their traditional supporters that privatization of Social Security would not happen without a political war. The Campaign began issuing reports showing how women and minorities and lower income persons had benefited from the current Social Security system and challenged the economic assumptions of the privatizers.

The unions and senior advocates dedicated to the social insurance concept of the program looked for other solutions. They believed that the crisis was being manufactured and privatization was being presented as the only solution. The most common proposal for the program's defenders was to raise the cap on earnings subject to the payroll tax. It was only $68,000 in 1998. Raising the cap completely would solve the entire problem of future shortfalls. Raising to $90,000 to $100,000 would solve a part of the problem.

The nation's economy continued to hum along at a remarkable growth rate. The Social Security Trustees issued their annual report on the fiscal health of the Trust Fund. In 1998, they extended the date of solvency to 2032. In 1999, with the economy still booming, the date was extended by five more years to 2037 and in 2000 it was extended to 2039.

In 1999, President Clinton issued his own proposal, which called for a new USA, Universal Savings Accounts, on top of Social Security, which would not replace guaranteed benefits. President Clinton and later Vice President Al Gore as the Democratic Presidential nominee in 2000 proposed using government surpluses to pay down the national debt and credit interest savings to Social Security.

New York State was considered key to efforts to fight privatization. With Republicans having a six seat edge in the House of Representatives, New York had 13 Republicans, most of whom were moderates and some like Congressman Jack Quinn of Buffalo with strong labor support.

StateWide organized a post card campaign against privatization. In 1999, the new Social Security Public Education Project sponsored a series of forums across the state with presentations by the Economic Policy Institute in Washington. Seniors like StateWide's President Ruby Sills Miller played an important role by relating about how she became disabled in her 50s by a stroke and she had to rely on Social Security:

"There is no doubt that Social Security is a family program, not just for retirees but for all generations. I know this first hand in my own family. On May 19, 1973, at the age of 53, I fell coming out of the Post Office. This changed by life drastically and I became a Social Security beneficiary before I became a senior citizen...I lost my speech and ability to read and write. My doctors thought I would not be able to return to work. During my prolonged rehabilitation, my Social Security disability benefits helped to sustain me for two and a half years, plus nine months after I returned to a very low-wage job."

The threat of privatization loomed even bigger in 2000 when Republican Presidential nominee George W. Bush made privatization a major issue of his campaign. In his acceptance speech at the Republican Convention in Philadelphia, he acknowledged the conventional wisdom was that Social Security was the "third rail" of Americans politics and you shouldn't touch it.

Bush talked generally about letting workers invest part of their own retirement money, but he didn't discuss what steps would be needed to pay the transition costs to this system. He argued that the Clinton administration had been unable to provide the leadership to enact change, but that he would be a leader working with both parties who could.

CHAPTER FOURTEEN

ON THE MARCH AGAIN: FIGHTING HMOS AND DRUG COMPANIES

HMOS BEGAN RECRUITING SENIORS AND OFFERING THEM SOME extra services not covered by Medicare including prescription drugs, eyeglasses and hearing aids, for example. They even offered a zero premium plan in some urban parts of the state. HMOs launched a big recruitment boom in New York after the Medicare changes enacted in the late 1990's. By 1998, over twelve percent of all New York seniors, mostly downstate, had joined.

HMOs might be okay for those who didn't have serious health problems but they were reversing traditional financial incentives. Since HMOs were paid a fixed amount, they were reversing a system in which the more health care providers did, the more they got paid to one in which the less they did the more they got to keep.

We talked about how HMOs were trying to recruit healthy, younger seniors who played golf and spent winters traveling rather than the 85-year-old who went into the hospital once or twice a year.

We argued there was no way HMOs could make a lot of money by being more economical or efficient because the Medicare population was older, kept aging and is expensive to care for. Even younger seniors with limited health problems, quickly aged into an older, more needy category.

In 1999, the bust came and over the next four years, they dropped coverage for nearly 200,000 older New Yorkers by simply terminating their plans in certain counties. They blamed the government for not providing sufficient reimbursements in those counties. Some studies showed though that HMOs altogether were costing Medicare more money than they were saving because they had "creamed" off so many relatively healthier seniors who cost less than average and left the more expensive ones in the traditional Medicare program.

In 1998, the lack of prescription drug coverage and the high cost of drugs again became a source of complaints in the state and mushroomed into one of the dominant public issues of the coming national campaign. It was precipitated largely by the first wave of cutbacks by Medicare HMOs, which decided to abandon certain counties in the state, which they viewed as not profitable. In late 1998, several HMOs announced they were pulling out of many counties in the suburbs around New York City. Outraged seniors in Orange County and Westchester County who had gotten used to the extra benefits including prescription drug coverage took their concerns to state legislators. They wanted action to increase the EPIC program by expanding income guidelines.

In the winter of 1999, a group of seniors in Orange County came to Albany and were presented at a press conference by Senate Democrats. They endorsed legislation sponsored by Senator Vincent Gentile, a young new senator who was on the Aging committee, to expand EPIC's income guidelines to $30,000 for a single senior and $35,000 for a couple. The income guidelines had been $18,500 for a single senior and $24,400 for a couple.

Action for further changes on EPIC seemed unlikely because the Legislature had made some modest changes to the program in 1998 that cost the state more money and raised income guidelines slightly to account for cost of living adjustments in Social Security which kept pushing current recipients over the maximum income levels.

Seniors led by Eve Encina of Warwick related how they had thousands of dollars of drug expenses and now had no HMO or private insurance coverage to pay for them. In April, a large group of seniors led by feisty Westchester County Legislator Bernice Spreckman hired several buses and met with the entire Westchester delegation in both houses.

The price of prescription drugs as well as EPIC expansion became a major issue as well. State Senator John Marchi introduced a bill in July 1999 that required the drug companies to give New York consumers the lowest rates they charged anywhere in the world. While the Marchi bill was not expected to be seriously considered, it became a rallying cry and organizing issue for StateWide and other groups.

CHAPTER FIFTEEN

GOODBYE ROSE

DURING THE LATER YEARS OF HER LIFE, ROSE RECEIVED MANY awards and honors. In 1996 Presbyterian Senior Services in New York gave its Maggie Kuhn Award to Rose Kryzak and an organization, Senior Action in a Gay Environment (SAGE), the first organization to serve older Lesbians and Gay men. In its program, Presbyterian Senior Services noted that Rose "is the leading spokesperson on aging in both the city and state...Rose, like Maggie Kuhn, attained prominence and public recognition as an advocate and leader after retirement."

In 1997, StateWide decided to honor Rose Kryzak while she was still living. At the organization's twenty-fifth anniversary dinner in June, it was announced that a new award was being named after her, the Rose Kryzak Advocacy Award. She delighted in this honor and was pleased to give the first award to Mike Bishansky of Rockland County that year and to Ruby Sills Miller of Manhattan and Barbara Hance of St. Lawrence County the next year. Though Rose became more frail and confined to a wheelchair, she still came to Albany for StateWide's board meetings and the annual convention every October. My wife and I always wondered as she left if we had seen her for the last time. She had aged, but if you closed your eyes and listened to her when she got the microphone, she still had that same strong advocate's voice summoning her peers to take needed actions.

In late June 1998, she came to Albany for StateWide's board meeting and she stayed at my home. I had long-planned to use my camcorder to videotape an oral history. So, I asked her to talk about her past. In addition to all the stories about Ellis Island, Social Security and senior issues, she also told me some things I had never heard before like how she had served lunch to Martin Luther King Jr. when he was a college student and friend of her neighbor's daughter who brought him home to Queens.

"Martin Luther King went to college with my neighbor's daughter. When they graduated, the neighbor didn't like the idea that her daughter was friendly with Martin Luther King. So, I said tell them to come and visit me. So, they did and instead of the mother, they introduced me to him. And, this girl was crazy about him and the parents I thought they would kill themselves....We had lunch in my house...A nice young man. They (the neighbors) knew that I could do different things!"

In October 1998, she came to the convention that marked the beginning of her hundredth year and was delighted with a drive to raise more money for the Rose Kryzak Legacy fund to honor her. That was what she lived for.

Board member Pat McArdle of Rockland County had heard about a program through the National Women's Hall of Fame in Seneca Falls New York that offered friends and families the opportunity to buy a plaque dedicated to a special woman in the their lives. Pat nominated Rose and she has her plaque displayed there.

By that time, Rose now was using a wheelchair all the time to get around. She was occasionally frustrated that she had some health problems that limited her, but she kept on working all the time. She was a realist too. She would always talk about the future but say, "*if* I am still here." Every year when the convention rolled around in the fall though, Rose was there in her wheelchair in the front of the meeting, still with the booming voice and the clear mind. As she got older, she was not always able to express herself as quickly and might forget a word she was thinking of, but she knew what she was trying to say. Her trips to Albany or other places would exhaust her and in her last years her family members were very concerned about her traveling. She would often come to a StateWide board meeting and have to take a nap during the afternoon. If she was fully rested, she was still very effective and able to participate.

The last time I saw her when she was active was in November 1998, right after StateWide's convention. I went to one of StateWide's regional meetings at the Community Church in Manhattan. Rose was there and as I sat back and listened, it struck me that Rose was sitting at the table out of the wheelchair. She had a red beret on and earrings and she was in fine form, fully participating in the meeting. I couldn't believe how well she looked since she wasn't tired from traveling like when she would be in Albany.

In early 1999, though, Rose was slowed by ailments and became frustrated that she wasn't able to do much. She had eye surgery in March. Then, in April, bleeding led to an examination that showed she had a tumor in her bladder. Even at the age of 99, she underwent the surgery, but was very weak and tired. Like always though, she was making plans to be active again. In a few weeks, StateWide's annual New York City garden party and fundraiser would take place in May at the home of her close friend Angela Fernandez. Rose came in her wheelchair and looked very frail, but those who attended said she held court and regaled in telling stories of past triumphs. It would be her final time at StateWide event.

I got a phone call later in May that Rose Kryzak was terminally ill with cancer. That evening, I got a call from her granddaughter that the visiting nurses gave her only 48 hours to live because she was bleeding internally quite heavily.

I thought about driving with my whole family to Queens the next day but decided it was an awfully long trip from Albany for the kids in one day and they had school on Monday. So, on a rainy Monday, the 24th, I boarded Amtrak for the trip to Penn Station and then got the Port Washington line of the Long Island Railroad to Main Street in Flushing. I walked a couple blocks to the Flushing House, the senior citizens' apartment building Rose had lived in for over a decade.

She was sleeping for 22 to 23 hours a day though she could be roused. Her granddaughter told her I was there and I went into her bedroom and she came to life, telling me they had raised $900 at their annual garden party just two weeks earlier. After we spoke for a few moments, I suggested she should get some rest. As I was walking out of her bedroom, she called out for me to get some lunch from the refrigerator. That was Rose.

I spent time talking with her granddaughter, Jeannie, and then her daughter Ann arrived with her husband from Florida. I went back to see her a few hours later before I left and we had a good talk. She asked about my children, my wife and mother.

The hours and days went by and we waited imminently for her to go into a coma. In typical fashion, she seemed to rally. By Thursday, when I expected she'd be in a coma, I called and her daughter said she wanted to talk with me. Rose got on the line and said, "Michael, I'm feeling better, I'm coming to the board meeting," which was a month later in Albany.

I kept calling every day save perhaps two when we went out of town for a day. She kept hanging on. The visiting nurses couldn't figure it out. Gradually though, after a couple of weeks, she began to be less responsive. She was still hanging on when our Board met on June 22 and 23 but the next morning, one month after I had seen Rose, I got a call from Lani Sanjek of our staff in New York at 6:30 with the long dreaded news. Rose had died during the night. That night, saddened I remember looking at the clear sky in the west as the sun was going down and thinking that for the first time in almost 100 years, the sun was setting on this planet and Rose Krzyak was no longer with us.

The *Associated Press* reported Rose's death and I read the story in the *Newark Star Ledger* the next day while I was visiting my in-laws. A few days later, the *New York Times* ran an obituary that called her "a vigorous advocate" for the elderly, and spent considerable time discussing her Communist Party involvement.

Her funeral was held three days later at the Swartz Memorial Chapel. Almost 200 persons attended. Kate and I left the kids in New Jersey and we took the drive to the funeral, over Staten Island, through Bay Ridge and Brooklyn until we arrived at Queens Boulevard and the Swartz Memorial Chapel at 76th Road. Jane Gould was the first person we saw, standing just inside the door as we arrived. The funeral looked like an old StateWide advocates meeting.

Rose's daughter Ann was the first speaker and said, "I came here to celebrate the life of a great woman, my mother, a Twenty-First century woman." Jane Gould called her a "role model to me," and she quoted Mario Cuomo saying, "Every time I see her, it costs me a few million dollars." Public Advocate Mark Green, remarked, " I get paid for being a public advocate. Rose was a public advocate without getting a cent for it. Her example should inspire us."

Bill Davis, speaking for the Communist Party, recalled her first public struggle with the utilities and said, "Yes, there is a 'Kryzak Problem'," it's just that there are not enough Rose Kryzaks. The world needs more, many more."

When I spoke, I repeated to her friends there what I end many talks I give to senior citizens' groups.

"When you think that the American political system is hopeless, that the little people can't make changes, that it is not worth trying, just remember a short little woman in her 90's who rose before dawn on many mornings to board a bus from New York to Albany to go to the State Capitol to fight for the people. She believed that even one person could make a difference, and she did."

I left with the same feeling of being moved and blessed but also of sadness and emptiness I felt when I left my grandmother's funeral over twenty years earlier.

"Yes, she may have been tiny but she was a giant," someone in the audience remarked. It was when she was interviewed for the documentary on the Communist Party, *Seeing Red*, that she made one of her memorable statements about feeling like she was a big person, not a little nothing. That was the video clip we used later that week to conclude a memorial service we held in Albany for seniors and persons in the field of aging. Then we lit candles, which had been distributed to everyone.

After Rose's death, Flushing House and the Queens Interagency Council on Aging joined StateWide in establishing awards in Rose's name. Flushing House gave out the first Rose Kryzak Senior Leadership Awards in November 2000. One of the winners, Anne Canadeo, director of resident services at Flushing House, worked with Rose on her last project, the Safe Shopping Program in Flushing. "She was forever thinking of new ways to make life easier and better for the elderly," Canadeo said.

In October, when Rose would have become 100 years old, StateWide held a special tribute to Rose at our annual convention which was dedicated to her. We had made a special videotape of her life and her nieces Barbara and Lucy along with granddaughters Jeannie and Becky attended. Lucy spoke and said she looked forward to carrying on her aunt's legacy in the years ahead. Five members of StateWide read vignettes from her life that were in Rose's own words. Helen Quirini, the leader of the General Electric retirees in Schenectady who had stood up to Chairman Jack Welch and vigorously advocated for higher pensions for long-time retirees, was given the Rose Kryzak Award.

Each year, StateWide holds a special Rose Kryzak Forum in October at the Community Church in Manhattan to discuss important advocacy issues.

CHAPTER SIXTEEN

ON OTHERS SHOULDERS: CARRYING ON THE LEGACY

IT SEEMED SO IRONIC THAT THE ISSUE OF PRESCRIPTION DRUGS WAS in the headlines at the time of Rose's death. In fact, just the week before, at StateWide's board meeting, StateWide members had gone home with an assignment to survey drugstores across the state in order to develop a list of prices that would be compared to prices in Canada. StateWide had been contacted by Public Citizen, the national consumer group in Washington, to help in its nationwide project to survey drugs prices. Public Citizen would analyze surveys completed by seniors from across the state and produce results according to an expert methodology. They were linking up with senior and consumer groups in many states across the country to do similar surveys.

Throughout the summer of 1999, seniors in New York from StateWide, JPAC and other organizations went to local drugstores and asked their pharmacists to fill-in the prices of the ten most commonly used drugs. Results were received from over 140 drugstores. Seniors also spent the summer collecting their own drug receipts and those of their friends. Thousands of them were mailed to the StateWide Albany office and *Newsday* showed a picture of them in a special story they did in October on drug prices and seniors' bus trips to Canada to buy cheaper drugs.

On November first at an Albany press conference, the final survey results were released and showed that New York seniors paid 106% more than Canadians for those ten drugs. The story got extensive coverage for Public Citizen and StateWide and drew further attention to the issue and to a bill sponsored by Maine Congressman Thomas Allen which would have allowed Medicare recipients to buy prescription drugs at the prices state Medicaid programs paid.

2000 loomed as a critical election year both in New York State and in Washington and it was again a year ending in a "0". The power to draw the district lines has been a partisan power that, more than any other factor, has allowed the Republicans to control the State Senate for every year except one since 1940 and the Democrats to control the Assembly continuously since 1974. Following the 1998 elections, Democrats controlled the 150 seat Assembly by a 98-52 margin and Republicans had an edge of 36-25 in the Senate.

Most Albany political analysts consider it almost impossible for either party to lose enough seats to cost them control of the house. Very few incumbents are ever defeated in state legislative races. Yet, Senate Republicans were worried somewhat by storm clouds on the horizon. A rebellion against Nassau County Republicans on Long Island had resulted in Democrats winning control of the county Legislature there for the first time in decades. Also, the arrival of Hillary Clinton as a candidate for the US Senate coupled with a presidential race in which Democrats could be expected to win the state easily could hurt Republican candidates on every ballot line.

State Senate Majority Leader Joseph Bruno made a calculated effort to move to the center and even the left in the 2000 legislative session, embracing programs and bills which were supported by liberal constituencies. In the 2000 session, Senate Republicans finally passed the hate crimes bill which increased penalties for violent crimes based on race, religion and sexual orientation. The Senate Republicans had always opposed this bill the Assembly passed annually because it included the special protections for gays and lesbians. In 2000, that changed.

Bruno had also met with the seniors from Orange County at the end of the 1999 legislative session in the spring and promised some action to expand EPIC to cover those with higher incomes. However, no additional funding made it into the final budget agreement for 1999-2000. Bruno and Senate Aging Chairman George Maziarz and others had held private discussions over the summer and Bruno decided that a massive expansion of the EPIC program would be another cornerstone of Senate Republican budget priorities in the 2000 legislative session. His chief budget advisor, Abe Lackman, developed a proposal to increase EPIC income guidelines to $35,000 for individual seniors and $50,000 for couples. Maziarz became an effective champion as Chair of the Aging Committee and he advocated with Bruno for the expansion.

I was at a meeting on state fiscal issues when I got an important call in November from Senator Maziarz who was at an airport. He told me of the Bruno plan and that it would be announced in the next few days. He told me that Abe Lackman would invite me to meet with him and review the proposal. I spoke to Abe and urged him to include the AARP as well so he and the staff briefed Bill Ferris of the AARP and me. We were concerned about whether the entire program would be paid for by tobacco money which would come at the expense of health care programs for other populations. Abe agreed that some money would come from the regular state budget. We agreed to join Bruno and many Senators at a press conference to endorse the concept of the expansion. It was a welcome and unexpected alliance that strengthened our relationship with Senate Republicans, in marked contrast to our targeting the Senate during the final days of passing the original EPIC bill.

Bruno knew that big action was needed on EPIC in order to help Senator Morahan win a rematch in his Orange and Rockland counties district. Morahan, a county legislative leader, had won a special election in May by a narrow margin and he had promised he would push for EPIC expansion. The Orange County seniors had him on videotape making that pledge. So, Morahan was named the prime sponsor of the bill and he became a genuine champion of the cause and worked closely with StateWide's members in Rockland County. The Republicans put the bill on the agenda and passed in on January 31. In the floor debate, Democrats argued over whose idea the EPIC expansion was and who should get the credit, noting that Senator Vincent Gentile had first proposed EPIC expansion.

Senator George Maziarz took the floor and said, "There's one person who quite frankly really deserves a whole lot more credit than (Democrats) Senator Gentile or Senator Dollinger, who thinks he deserves a lot of credit for it, and anybody else over there or even more credit than Senator Morahan. And that is the late Rose Kryzak, who passed away last year at the ripe age of 99 years old...it was really Rose Kryzak and the New York State Senior Action Council that really brought the EPIC program about here in New York State. So we may disagree today on who deserves credit for it, and I'm sure that when the mailings go out we're all going to disagree on who gets the credit for it. But the one person who really deserves an awful lot of credit, is the late Rose Kryzak."

Later, Senator Toby Stavisky, a New York City Democrat who had recently replaced her deceased husband Leonard as a Senator, added,

"I commend Senator Maziarz for mentioning the name of Rose Kryzak. Rose, who if she had been elected to the Legislature, I assure you she would have been sitting on this side of the aisle, Rose Kryzak was a remarkable woman...She was an old Socialist and she was a very good friend of mine. And I'm proud today to cast my vote with Rose Kryzak in mind."

Meanwhile, the Assembly mulled over how to respond to a Republican-dominated Senate trying to outflank it on a program the Assembly had always felt it authored. Assembly staff vowed that the Senate would never outspend them on EPIC and they said they were preparing a plan that might even be ready in a special session in December, shades of 1986 again. However, the leadership and the staff did not respond then or even when the Senate passed their bill on January 31. The staff said they would rather develop a good proposal than just get one out quickly. Finally, they came up with their proposal as they were ready to pass their own budget resolution in March. It spent over $300 million and was more generous than the Senate plan, especially for lower income seniors. In budget negotiations though between the governor's staff and both houses, the Assembly quickly abandoned the huge size of its proposal and agreed to a more modest $125 million program expansion.

Though Governor Pataki later tried to take credit for signing the bill and featured himself in advertising the expanded program, his staff and the Division of the Budget had not offered their own ideas on the expansion other than when State Health Commissioner Antonia Novello, the former US Surgeon General under President Reagan, testified at a budget hearing in February that the federal government ought to provide coverage under Medicare. As in the 1980's under Cuomo, the Division of the Budget began pushing for changes to restrict the cost of the program. At first DOB proposed huge deductibles for new participants that would have forced seniors with $20,000 annual income to pay $1000 in drugs costs before getting any assistance. That idea was thrown out but Pataki and DOB insisted that there was too much spending in the current budget. They wanted the start of EPIC and some other programs delayed until January 1, 2001 rather than October 1, 2000. StateWide objected in the media and kept up the fight to the annoyance of legislative staff. Finally, the budget was passed in May and the EPIC expansion was included with the income eligibility increases up to $35,000 and $50,000 and reduced fees for the lower income persons in a two-tiered system of premiums and deductibles that increased with income.

StateWide joined with Mae Carpenter, the Director of the Westchester County Office for the Aging, and Bernice Spreckman, a county legislator and senior leader there, and eighteen other local groups including JPAC, Citizen Action, the Hispanic Senior Action Council and many unions and brought 500 persons to Albany for a Grassroots Senior Citizens Day on May 2. This event that also served as a tribute for retiring Assemblyman Paul Harenberg, the co-sponsor of the original EPIC program and the "Claude Pepper" of New York State's Legislature. Bruno and Silver both spoke to the group on that day and expressed their desire to have the program start in October. The deal had already been sealed though and just a few hours later on that day, it became clear that the program probably wouldn't start until January.

Even with the existing guidelines, 1500 more people were signing up for EPIC every month and the expanded program would about double the number of enrollees in 2001, the first year changes went into effect. In Washington, the argument over prescription drug coverage under Medicare would take center stage in the 2000 Presidential election campaign.

CHAPTER SEVENTEEN

"MAPLE POWER:
PEACE, LOVE, AND CHEAP DRUGS"

IN MAY 2000, PUBLIC CITIZEN IN WASHINGTON APPROACHED
StateWide about co-sponsoring a bus trip to Montreal that would
allow seniors to buy cheaper drugs and also provide an opportunity for New York's US Senate candidates to join the ride and
announce support of the Kennedy-Allen bill. StateWide had been
considering how it could take seniors on buses to Canada. One
prospect was to take them to a pharmacy on the Canadian side of
the St. Regis Indian Reservation which straddled the New York-
Canadian border. However, the pharmacist there wasn't prepared
for a busload of Americans. A doctor in Ogdensburg who had a
Canadian license and who could prescribe drugs to be filled over
the border also didn't want the media attention and the added rush
of business.

Taking bus trips to Canada had become a dramatic, grassroots
advocacy tool during the election year that had caught on, especially
after Mike Wallace had accompanied a bus trip from Maine in the
fall of 1999 for a story on *60 Minutes*. It wasn't long before most
Americans, to their surprise, became aware that prices for prescription drugs were much lower in Canada and that American
customers without insurance were being "price gouged" in the

view of many. The story snowballed and soon there were studies done by Congressman Tom Allen of Maine showing that not only did Canadians get lower prescription drug prices, but so did pets. StateWide distributed a popular flyer that Greg Olsen developed to all legislators with a picture of a kindly-looking dog saying that "seniors were treated worse than dogs." Legislative staff howled in delight and the point was made and then repeated by legislators in their public remarks.

It was hoped that Hillary Clinton and her opponent New York City Mayor Rudolph Giuliani would get on board the bus. For almost a year Mrs. Clinton and Giuliani had been engaged in a campaign of political titans that was heading to a dramatic show-down in the fall.

New York's long-time Senator, Daniel Patrick Moynihan, announced in early 1999 that he would retire and not seek re-election in 2000. Immediately, there was speculation on who would run for his seat. State Comptroller Carl McCall was considered a front runner, but he decided he wasn't interested. He had his eye on running for governor in 2002. Andrew Cuomo, the Secretary of Housing and Urban Development and the son of the former governor, was another big name, but he was lining up to support Al Gore's presidential run and possibly have a key job in the administration if Gore won.

There began to be speculation that First Lady Hillary Rodham Clinton would run. Many dismissed the idea at first. After all, she didn't live in New York and she still was living in the White House. Mrs. Clinton was approached by Democratic leaders in the state including Congressman Charles Rangel and didn't rule out the idea. In the spring of 1999, she had just soldiered through the humiliation of President Clinton's impeachment and the Monica Lewinsky sex scandal. Many thought she was ready to start her own political career and make history.

Within a few months, she was at Moynihan's Delaware County farm upstate near Oneonta, getting the Senator's blessing and yes, she was off and running. She started with listening tours in many parts of the state where she would take notes while discussing issues with local people. Many in New York didn't like her and thought she was a carpetbagger, including many Democrats. However, by May 2000 when the State Democratic convention would nominate her in Albany she had traveled to small towns all over upstate New York and many local people appreciated her attention and the hard work and effort they saw her making. Hillary obliged as thousands of New Yorkers asked to have their picture taken with her.

For example, in Massena on the Canadian border where my relatives lived, her visit was a big community event. Mayor Charlie Boots had her as a guest for a party at his home. People lined the street near his house while she was there. Some of my other relatives got their pictures taken with her.

The Democratic Party wanted her nomination to be fitting for an historic candidacy of a First Lady. Never before had a president's wife run for the Senate. So, the party leaders decided to hold the convention at Albany's Pepsi Arena which could hold at least 15,000 persons. They opened the event to the public. Everyone wondered whether the president would come and take part. He wasn't on the early schedule. But on the day of her nomination, Air Force One landed in Albany and Hillary Clinton's nomination included her husband on the platform.

The convention was nearly as spectacular as the national party conventions with 11,500 people attending and it ended with a balloon drop and a rain of confetti to the music of *Chariots of Fire*. It was shown on all the national networks.

Mrs. Clinton traveled all over the state. Giuliani had not seemed too engaged and didn't make too many upstate visits. Then, in May two bombshells hit and Giuliani decided to leave the race. He announced he had prostate cancer and acknowledged he had a female companion and was virtually estranged from his wife. His public image had sunk to a new low. By the end of May when the Republicans met to nominate their candidate, Giuliani had bowed out and Long Island Congressman Rick Lazio quickly jumped into the race. Lazio had been planning to run and even challenge Giuliani in a primary until top leaders led by Governor Pataki urged him to defer to the Mayor.

StateWide sent invitations to Mrs. Clinton and to Lazio to join the bus trip but they didn't. The trip proved to be very difficult to organize. While there were many seniors who could not afford their prescription drugs, some were too frail to travel on the bus overnight. One senior near Saratoga Springs was eager to go but was confined to a wheelchair and was too sick to go. Others couldn't go on short notice or on the days when the trip was planned, June 5-6.

The arrangements also proved difficult. Ever since the October bus trip with *60 Minutes*, the Canadian government was keeping a more watchful eye on Canadian pharmacies so that they didn't violate the Canadian law, which required that prescriptions only be filled if written by a Canadian doctor. And, the doctor should actually examine the patient. The Montreal pharmacy in the *60 Minutes* story didn't fill prescriptions written by American doctors and got into unwelcome trouble. The pharmacies were also leery of the buses because the *60 Minutes* coverage created a media circus that disrupted the pharmacy. So, the staff of Public Citizen didn't want details of the visit to be made public. We couldn't discuss the name of the doctor who was going to briefly examine, without charge, all of the patients. Also, we couldn't mention where we were going to stay which was at a convent in the Westmount section of Montreal where almost all the nuns were elderly and only spoke French.

I was very worried because there was a real chance that the trip would have to be canceled since there were few persons who were planning to go until the very end. Finally, about a dozen seniors mostly from Citizen Action's Binghamton chapter plus staff and film crews were signed up to go from Albany and the other bus leaving from Rochester which had been organized by Congresswoman Louise Slaughter would have about fifteen seniors.

The morning of Monday, June 5th was cloudy and very gray in Albany. A podium was set up under the State Street archway of the State Capitol. The Wade Tours bus pulled up and parked across the street. Two seniors ready to board the bus spoke along with Congressman Maurice Hinchey and State Senator John Marchi. The seniors from Binghamton brought signs. One proclaimed, "Maple Power: Peace, Love and Cheap Drugs." Greg Olsen of StateWide plastered the side of the bus with the thousands of drug receipts StateWide had collected. Four local television crews joined the trip. One crew came from Binghamton and then another from Albany's FOX station, rode the bus. As the bus crossed the border later that afternoon a crew from the Plattsburgh NBC affiliate met the Albany bus. The skies brightened and the sun came out as the buses arrived at the border. Canadian authorities ordered everyone out and each person was briefly interviewed before approved to head into Canada. Finally, the bus pulled into the convent in West Montreal and we dined in the dining hall with scores of elderly nuns.

That night everyone went back on the bus for a guided tour of the city with the Canadian doctor who had agreed to examine the

American seniors the next day. The next morning, Dr. Saba, who worked at McGill University and who had volunteered his service to help the American seniors began his exams in the morning and continued until early in the afternoon. The local New York television crews filmed the doctor and later conducted interviews with the seniors from their areas. Seventy-eight year-old Reggie Black had just moved to Albany a year earlier. He had been a seaman during his working days and now lived alone on a meager income. He had never bought one of this prescriptions in the United States because it cost too much, about $1,000. In Montreal, he paid about $300 for it. His story became the focus of the Albany FOX station's coverage and he was featured in Deborah Barfield's *Newsday* article. As the Fox station covered him being examined by Dr. Saba, Reggie started crying on camera, saying sometimes he didn't know if life was worth living. Later on the bus returning to Albany, he was more upbeat, happy that he got the prescriptions and talked about the need for a better health system in the United States that didn't make it necessary to go to Canada.

It was about 1:45 p.m. when the doctor had finished the medical exams. He and the seniors boarded the buses and went to the Uniprix pharmacy near the intersection of Peel Street and St. Catherine's in downtown Montreal where the pharmacists filled the prescriptions.

The group hoped to be back in Albany by dinner time. However, the process was long, especially with the reporters filming most of the transactions. The seniors were very happy with the huge savings at the pharmacy, realizing that all those media stories about Canadian drug prices were true. Public Citizen compiled a list of their savings on this trip which showed that they paid $177.54 in Canada for Zocor instead of $303.96 in the United States, $40.92 for Glucophage instead of $127.95, $63.36 for Lipitor instead of

$98.25, $98.34 for Vioxx instead of $195.84, $128.70 for Evista instead of $174.00.

It wasn't until the rush hour that the group boarded the bus outside the pharmacy for the return trip that spent an hour in city traffic and then turned into a long drive on a rainy night, arriving back in Albany about 11:00 p.m. Many of the seniors were living on limited incomes and obviously had high health costs. Several were going to drive back to Binghamton in the middle of the night but StateWide and Public Citizen agreed to pay for four motel rooms and everyone stayed in Albany until the next morning. Like any traveling adventure, a camaraderie developed among us all, including the reporters, in just thirty-six hours together.

These bus trips to Canada became a cause celebre for politicians and candidates in states all across the Canadian border during the summer and fall. Buses were leaving from Montana, Michigan, Minnesota and other states. Brian Schweitzer, the Democratic Senate candidate in Montana, paid for the bus trip and reaped tremendous favorable media coverage. He nearly upset incumbent Conrad Burns. Minnesota Senator Mark Dayton had also been funding bus trips by the Minnesota Senior Federation. The pharmaceutical industry sponsored a front group, Citizens for Better Medicare, that had begun spending millions on media commercials that were intended to undercut these candidates and the reformers. In Michigan they spent millions criticizing the Canadian system of universal health care or "socialized medicine" as the drug companies liked to say, the same tired argument doctors had used in fighting Medicare in the mid-1960's.

By the fall, a full blitz of TV ads in upstate New York showed a fictitious bus of Canadians heading south as refugees because they couldn't get treated in Canada. Of course, that distorted the issue because there were no buses of Canadians coming to the

United States to buy prescription drugs but Pharma, the Pharmaceutical Manufacturers Association, wanted to argue that problems in the Canadian health care system were, in their view, causing rationed health care and some Canadians to seek treatment in the United States.

The bus refugees role in the US election campaign became a matter of international interest as StateWide had calls from French and Japanese television networks wanting to accompany any further bus trips to Canada StateWide might be planning.

Social Security, Medicare and prescription drug prices and coverage became central issues of the 2000 presidential campaign during the summer and fall. Vice President Al Gore adopted a populist tone, charging that Governor George W. Bush would harm Social Security and he took the offensive announcing his prescription drug program late in August. Bush seemed on the defensive on the issue but he decided to compete for the senior vote and he offered his own prescription drug coverage proposal and attacked Gore's as more big government. Gore used the prescription drug issue as a major centerpiece of his campaign. Bush turned the tables on him though by raising questions about a mis-statement Gore made about Gore's mother's prescription drugs. Bush cast it as another matter of whether Gore was fudging the truth and whether he could be trusted. Gore's momentum was interrupted by a number of charges like those Bush made in September. Bush was able to "muddle" the prescription drug issue enough to assure seniors he was an advocate and make in-roads with seniors who generally supported Democrats on the issue. Most exit polls would show that Gore won the senior vote by a small margin though Bush had an edge in the decisive state of Florida.

Meanwhile, one week before the election, StateWide's twenty-ninth annual convention opened in Albany on October 30th. Hillary

Clinton and Congressman Lazio had been invited months earlier to attend but Lazio had declined. Four days before the convention began, Hillary Clinton's staff confirmed that she would accept StateWide's invitation and speak just after it began at 1:15 in the afternoon. Chelsea came with her, beginning the last week of the election campaign.

A throng of media also came with her. StateWide arranged to highlight Social Security and Medicare issues right before she spoke. During the late summer and fall, StateWide had joined with the Campaign for America's Future in a national effort to get Congressional and Senatorial candidates to sign a pledge that they would not privatize Social Security and Medicare. Hillary Clinton had agreed to sign the pledge in September. StateWide had pushed her and Congressman Lazio all summer to sign it. Lazio refused. Mrs. Clinton's staff said she would but hadn't done so. So, StateWide issued a press release in mid-September criticizing both for not doing so. Within 24 hours, Hillary Clinton signed a copy of the pledge and faxed it back to StateWide's office. At the October convention, Roger Hickey, Executive Director of the Campaign for America's Future, flew in from Washington to speak about the pledge and watch as Mrs. Clinton symbolically signed it again in Albany.

Speaking right before Mrs. Clinton was 58-year-old Brenda Harper, a disabled woman from Clay in central New York. She had contacted StateWide after seeing a Syracuse newspaper story about how the organization was helping people with information about buying drugs in Canada. StateWide urged her to come to Albany and speak to Mrs. Clinton. Mrs. Harper related how she had several health problems and prescriptions for her and her husband were costing them over a $1200 a month. At 58 she would not be eligible for the expanded EPIC program. She told Mrs.

Clinton and those attending the convention that she was in danger of losing her home because they couldn't afford the drugs and the mortgage.

Hillary Clinton addressed Social Security, Medicare, prescription drugs and long-term care when she spoke. Prescription drugs had become an important issue for her in the campaign. She had unveiled a plan to allow drugs to be imported from Canada. As Michael Tomasky reported in his book *Hillary's Turn,*

"At a Rochester hospital, the message was prescription drug prices. Mentioning the far lower prices for many drugs in Canada, and arguing for their importation, went down well in a city so near the Canadian border; I noticed at least a half-dozen people who had not even applauded when she was introduced joining the standing ovation when she finished."

The visit of Hillary and Chelsea Clinton was a great moment in StateWide's history and a testament to the power of a citizens' group to influence public affairs. Rose Kryzak would have loved the event and given Hillary her thoughts and her advice on the issues. Rose's spirit was in the room though.

Eight days later, Mrs. Clinton was elected to be New York's junior Senator and 36 days later the presidential election was finally settled by the Supreme Court and George W. Bush was determined to be the forty-third President of the United States. Domestic issues like prescription drugs, Medicare and Social Security continued to be hot button public issues in the early days of the Bush Administration - until September 11, 2001 when history intervened and like so many earlier times, domestic issues were pushed off the front pages, waiting to be addressed on another day.

EPILOGUE

I HAVE NO DOUBT THAT DEMOCRACY IS THE BEST SYSTEM OF government ever conceived. The freedom to make a better, more prosperous life without the fear of big government goes with it. That is why my grandparents came to this country. I also know though that democracy only works if the people work - work at making it function and responsive to the people, not just those who have donated to their campaigns.

What is this work? It is being diligent and following what happens locally, at the state level and nationally. More than that, it is community organizing to make government enact the changes we want, it is lobbying elected officials to propose legislation that will achieve what we seek. We have to vote. That is our chance to direct who will run our government. Unfortunately, between elections it is left to those who are active and organized and too often, paid lobbyists for private interests which make campaign donations have more influence than citizen-lobbyists working for the public interest.

The American way of government is about more than the freedom to vote though. It is about a struggle to make sure that America is not a country of disconnected individuals. It is more than that. It has been a great struggle to make America a "more perfect union." Rose and her generation saw that. At the time she came to America in 1910 women would not have the right to vote for another decade. For those of us who grew up in the 1960's, we saw it as African-Americans were denied the right to vote by literacy tests, poll taxes and hostile county registrars in the South. Now a new generation is finding their vote is losing its meaning because the weight of big money is being used to permeate every aspect of our political system which seems to be auctioned off to the highest bidder. The question is whether America's government will reflect the dream to serve the common good, not comfort the comfortable.

It is impossible to work alone. You have to join an organization like the AARP or StateWide or the League of Women Voters or the Sierra Club. And, organizations have to build coalitions because people with the same mission and goals often are in many different organizations.

Two years after Rose died, we had a special speaker at our 2001 convention in those dark days after September 11. Doris Haddock, like Rose, is active into her 90's. In fact, after the century came to a close and a new one ready to dawn, she chose to walk across America at age 90 as a statement and a rallying call for campaign finance reform, the McCain-Feingold bill. She believed in America and the power of one person joining with many others to make change and force a big powerful government to have to respond.

Despite emphysema and arthritis, "Granny D" made it to Washington, cross country skiing along the Potomac for the last stretch. She was welcomed as a hero at the Capitol by John McCain and others. There, before she was arrested, she gave one of the most brilliant speeches I have ever read.

"This morning we began our walk among the graves of Arlington, so that those spirits, some of whom may be old friends, might join us today and that we might ask of them now, 'Did you brave spirits, give your lives for a government where we might

stand together as free and equal citizens, or did you give your lives so that laws might be sold to the highest bidder, turning this temple of our fair republic into a bawdy house where anything and everything is done for a price?'

After her arrest for trespassing at the Capitol, she spoke before Judge Hamilton in the court:

"Your Honor, the old woman who stands before you was arrested for reading the Declaration of Independence in America's Capitol Building. I did not raise my voice to do so and I blocked no hall... Your Honor, it is now your turn to be a part of this arrest. If your concern is that we might have interfered with the visitor's right to a meaningful tour of the Capitol, I tell you that we helped them have a more meaningful one. If your concern is that we might have been blocking the halls of our government, let me assure you that we stood to one side of the Rotunda where we would not be in anyone's way. But I inform you that the halls are indeed blocked over there.

They are blocked by the shameless sale of public policy to campaign contributors, which bars the doors and the halls to the people's legitimate needs and the flow of proper representation. We Americans must put an end to it in any peaceful way that we can. Yes, we can speak when we vote, and we do. But we must also give our best effort to encourage the repair of a very broken system. We must do both....

In my 90 years, this is the first time I have been arrested. I risk my good name, for I do indeed care what my neighbors think about me. But, Your Honor, some of us do not have much power, except to put our bodies in the way of an injustice, to picket, to walk or to just stand in the way. It will not change the world overnight, but it is all we can do."

Rose Kryzak would have loved to meet Doris Haddock, a kindred spirit. We Baby Boomers, the next generation of senior activists, will be standing on their shoulders.

New York StateWide
Senior Action Council Board Members

The following list is as complete as available in Statewide's archives.

New York City

Annie Bowen
Alma Harper
Beatrice Jackson
Rose Kryzak
Ruby Sills Miller
Pearl Reeves
Clara Stanton
Leon Von Holden
Ruth Whitted
Walter Woods

Long Island
Rev. Winston Anderson
Brigitte Castellano
James Connolly
Thomas Doherty
Concetta Forte
McIvaine Harris
Annie Morgan
John Patterson

Lower Hudson Valley
Mike Bishansky
Edmund Braun
Beatrice Halloran
Ruth Hawes
Bernard Jacobs
Margaret Mary King
Pat McArdle
Rose Pierce
Olive Rejmaniak

Charles Tanner
Myrtle Von Helmolt
Melvin Woolheater
Moses Zuckerman

Central/Leatherstocking
Emil Grocholl
Pauline Kinney
Edward Mack
Ed Nichols
Amber Scholz
Henry Shearer
Charlotte Springer
Delvin Sullivan
Edith Warren
Doris Wood

Capital District
Hank Antonelli
Sophie T. Barber
Gertrude Champagne
Donald Collins
Rev. John Edmond
Rev. Howard Hills
Elizabeth Jones
William Michalski
Thomas Miller
Rhoda Murray
Helen Quirini
Sybil Robertson
Michael Widzowski

North Country
Margaret Cuthbert
Lawrence Fregoe
Mary Hair
Albert Lawrence
Robert Miller
Sister Margaret Mary McMullen
Charles Nindl
Anna Premo
Joseph Sears
Alice Van Sickle

Central New York
Marge Bennett
Francis Benton
Grace Eggleston
John Flesack
Sarah King
Margaret Klotz
Deforest Pangburn
Florence Smith
Albert Woodard

Southern Tier
Dorothy Brownell
Walter Davis
Frances Hannon
Robert Hill
Mamye Joy
Alice Logan
William Luzier
Willis White

Rochester/Finger Lakes
Jeannette Clingerman
Willard Crosier
Mary Hawkins
Robert Judson
George Kreger
Sophia Loveless
Vernon Loveless
Robert Maier
Marge Molloy
Robert Renner
Leon Roets
William Taggart
Helen Wood

Erie/Niagara
Max Berman
Minnie Brown
Curtis Buckley
Arta Davis
Peter Frensch
James Jackson
Josephine Nowak
Alice Roeder
Ollie Scott
Betty Smith
Fran Staszak
Vladmir Vilus
Sigmund Wiechec
Peter Zanghi

ABOUT THE AUTHOR

MICHAEL BURGESS turned 50 years old on October 2, 2003 and became a member of the New York StateWide Senior Action Council, twenty-five years after he began his association with the organization as a consultant on energy issues in 1979. Three years later he became Executive Director for five years (1982-87) and in 1995 returned to the position he still holds.

Mike has played a major role in many pieces of legislation effecting older New Yorkers. He played a leading role in the lobbying and organizing effort that led to the passage of the EPIC (Elderly Pharmaceutical Insurance Coverage) program in 1986 and was involved in advocating for the major expansion of the program in 2000. By September 2003, over 322,000 older New Yorkers are EPIC beneficiaries, making it the largest senior prescription drug in the nation. He has become a leading consumer voice on prescription drug pricing issues and has appeared on CNN Fn "Your Money," National Public Radio's "Marketplace," "Inside Albany" and many local and regional media outlets. He helped organize and participated in a bus trip to Montreal Canada in June 2000 to help older New Yorkers buy more affordable prescription drugs.

Mike has written numerous op-ed pieces and articles which have appeared in the *Albany Times-Union, Newsday* and *Empire State Reports*. As Director of the Non-Profit Resource Center, he provided advocacy training to nonprofit organizations and edited the Citizens Guide to the New York State Legislature.

He also organized a new nonprofit organization, Community

Works of New York State, a fundraising federation of twenty-onelocal and statewide human services advocacy organizations which participates in workplace giving campaigns.

In 2002, he was elected to the Board of Directors of the national Alliance for Retired Americans (ARA).

Mike is a native of Massena in Northern New York. He grew up in Watertown, New York and graduated with a degree in Government from St. Lawrence University, Canton, New York, in 1975. He moved to Albany in 1979 and he currently lives in Delmar, outside Albany, with his wife, Kate, and children Joseph and Catherine.

To join the New York StateWide Senior Action Council
or for more information about the organization,
go to www.nysenior.org or call 518 436-1006

New York StateWide Senior Action Council,
275 State Street,
Albany, New York 12210